Charmaine Solomon's
Asian Favourites

Illustrations by Verity Prideaux • Photography by Greg Elms

A SUE HINES BOOK
ALLEN & UNWIN

First published in 2001

Copyright text © Charmaine Solomon 2001
Copyright illustrations © Verity Prideaux 2001
Copyright photography © Greg Elms 2001

A Sue Hines Book
Allen & Unwin Pty Ltd
83 Alexander Street
Crows Nest NSW 2065
Australia
Phone: (61 2) 8425 0100
Fax: (61 2) 9906 2218
Email: frontdesk@allen-unwin.com.au
Web: http://www.allenandunwin.com

National Library of Australia
Cataloguing-in-publication entry:

   1. Cookery, Asian. 2. Cookery, Oriental. I. Title.
   Solomon, Charmaine, 1930-.
   Charmaine Solomon's Asian Favourites.
   Includes index.
   ISBN 1 86508 140X.
   1. Cookery, Asian. 2. Cookery, Oriental. I. Title.

641.595

Designed by Mark Davis, text-art
Food prepared and styled by Virginia Dowzer
Bowls supplied by Freedom Furniture
Edited by Foong Ling Kong
Typeset by text-art
Index by Fay Donlevy
Printed by South China Printing Company, Hong Kong
10 9 8 7 6 5 4 3 2 1

To my busy family and friends who have enjoyed my cooking and given me a great appreciation of dishes which are universally popular. With love, I offer short cuts to traditional methods which result in no loss of flavour, and make it possible to cook a meal at home in the time available.

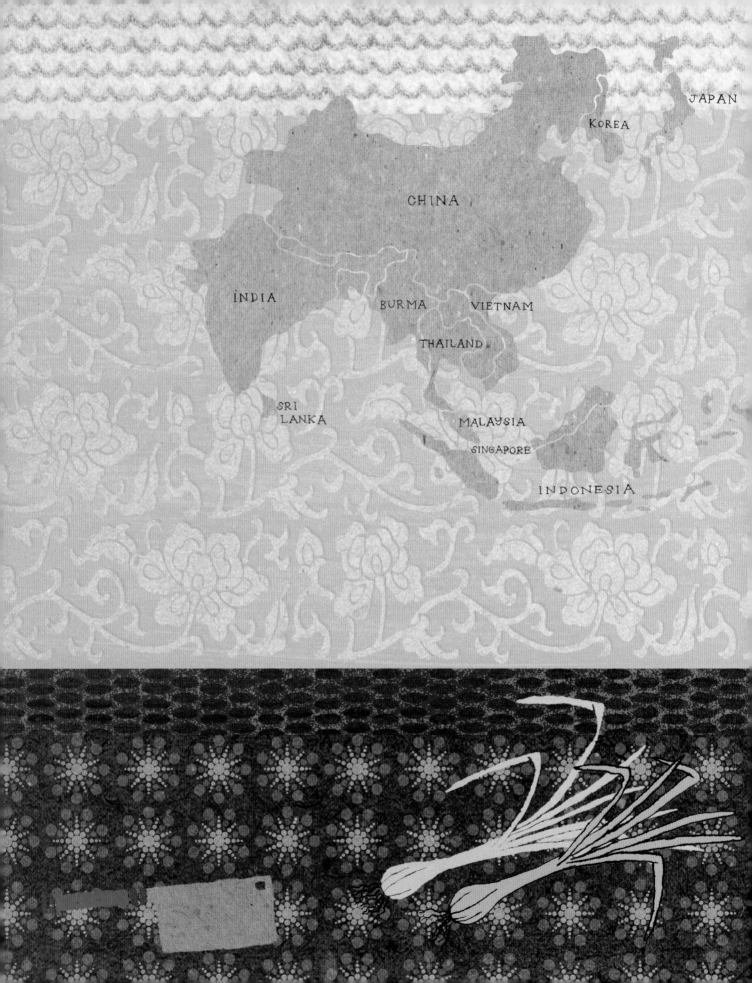

Contents

Conversion Tables

OVEN TEMPERATURES

150°C	300°F
180°C	350°F
200°C	400°F
230°C	450°F

WEIGHT MEASUREMENTS

50 g	1¾ oz
60 g	2 oz
100 g	3½ oz
125 g	4 oz
150 g	5 oz
160 g	5½ oz
200 g	7 oz
250 g	8 oz
300 g	10 oz
350 g	11 oz
375 g	12 oz
400 g	14 oz
500 g	1 lb
750 g	1½ lb
1 kg	2 lb
1.5 kg	3 lb
2 kg	4 lb

VOLUME MEASUREMENTS

60 ml	2 fl oz	¼ cup
100 ml	3½ fl oz	
125 ml	4 fl oz	½ cup
186 ml	6 fl oz	¾ cup
200 ml	7 fl oz	
250 ml	8 fl oz	1 cup
300 ml	10 fl oz	
375 ml	12 fl oz	1½ cup
400 ml	13 fl oz	
500 ml	16 fl oz	2 cups
560 ml	19 fl oz	
600 ml	20 fl oz	2½ cups
750 ml	24 fl oz	3 cups
825 ml	27 fl oz	3½ cups
1 lt	2 pints	4 cups
1.5 lt	3 pints	6 cups
2 lt	4 pints	8 cups

MEASURES

3 mm	⅛ in
1 cm	½ in
2 cm	¾ in
5 cm	2 in
15 cm	6 in
21.5 cm	8 in

Great Dishes of Asia

ALL OVER THE WORLD, tastebuds have been captured and held to ransom by the flavours of Asia. Affordable travel has introduced new flavours to timid palates. These are dishes you may have come across at restaurants, food stalls or in friends' homes.

Now the traveller wants to taste those flavours again without the cost of the fare. In big cities, a restaurant from any part of the world is sure to be found. I remember visiting Odense in Denmark and yearning for a simple Thai soup, with its clear and sharp flavours. In a Thai restaurant I was served this dish with all the fresh herbs and roots it would have featured in its native land. 'We fly them in every week,' the waiter said when I expressed surprise.

But what about those who do not live in big cities, or who would rather cook a meal at home? It can be done. The recipes here are typical of many Asian countries which have become famous for certain dishes. You will find soups, snacks and main meals in each country's repertoire.

Even the most delectable dish must be practical. What's the point of having a famous recipe and no time to work your way through it? I have to admit that some recipes scare me off—that pounding and grinding is all very well when there is domestic staff to help out, but in western lands this is the exception rather than the rule.

I have shared the time-saving methods I use in my own kitchen, taking the tedium out of preparation by offering helpful hints—such as making more of a spice blend than you need for a single meal and how to store it ready for the next time you want that particular experience. Or making a large pot of stock (something that cannot be hurried) and freezing it in portions of convenient size.

My hope is that you return to these recipes time and again, and enjoy the experience.

Thailand, Burma and Vietnam

AMONG THE SIMILARITIES in the food of these neighbouring lands is the abundant use of garlic and the fresh herb coriander.

Perhaps the most distinctive feature of Thai food is the liberal use of herbs such as mint, lemongrass, kaffir lime leaves, galangal, fresh chillies and the different varieties of basil. Thai curries are complex and offer many nuances of flavour. Traditionally, Thai food is cooked in pork fat, though for health reasons many cooks outside Thailand use vegetable oil.

Burmese food, on the other hand, is cooked in sesame oil and relies on the long, slow cooking of a purée of onion, garlic, ginger, turmeric and chilli. The mixture is cooked until the water content of the onions evaporates, leaving a richly flavoured mass with oil separating around the edges. It is this process that gives Burmese food its individuality, and is the most important step in preparing a Burmese curry. Fresh coriander, spring onions (scallions) and lemongrass are the most commonly used herbs. Burmese food reveals quite a bit of Indian influence, obvious in certain curries where spices such as cumin, coriander, cardamom or cloves are used in very small quantities— a subtle combination that adds fragrance to a curry. Burmese food is seldom heavy on chilli, unless in relishes.

Vietnamese food is not cooked in oil or fat as much as by steaming or boiling. It is also reliant on fresh herbs, and a large variety of them. At Vietnamese restaurants you are likely to be brought a plate of fragrant herbs to be added to your meal or eaten as a side salad. Soups are served with a meal, not as a separate course. The exception is the famous *pho* (pronounced 'far') of Vietnam, which is a full meal in a bowl.

I

In general, Thai soups are more piquant and strongly flavoured, while the soups of Burma and Vietnam are delicate. All three countries share a dependence on the strongly flavoured shrimp paste (*kapi* in Thailand, *ngapi* in Burma, *mam tom* in Vietnam), a little bit of which goes into almost every savoury dish. Fish sauce, too, is a staple in every kitchen, and Vietnamese fish sauce is said to be the best. When used in quantities specified, these two pungent ingredients will not obtrude their aroma or flavour in a dish but bring out the best in other foods.

Rice and noodles are staples in all three countries. The rice used is mainly polished white rice, and rice flour noodles of varying widths, both fresh and dried. Some meals also feature egg and wheat flour noodles. Bean starch noodles, sometimes called 'cellophane noodles' or 'spring rain noodles', are used for certain dishes.

Fresh ingredients may be bought as required, but growing a few herbs such as basil, coriander, spring onions (scallions) and lemongrass would not go amiss. Vietnamese mint (also known as Asian mint, hot mint, Cambodian mint or laksa leaf, but actually *polygonum odoratum*) is a rewarding herb to grow, because it is hardy and requires only a sunny spot and regular watering to grow into a fragrant patch. It is a most useful addition to tuck into a leaf parcel with Vietnamese spring rolls or to serve with Vietnamese *pho*.

For making the pastes and blends essential to Thai curries, a powerful electric blender is the most useful appliance. Either that, or find a heavy mortar and pestle, and develop a pounding technique!

A wok is indispensable for stir-fried dishes, but heavy saucepans are not to be scorned. Steaming baskets, too, are useful.

RECOMMENDED PANTRY

Black peppercorns
Chilli powder
Coconut milk, canned
Coriander, ground
Cumin, ground
Dried shrimp paste (*blacan*)
Dried tiny shrimps
Fish sauce
Galangal, fresh or bottled in brine

Noodles, dried
Palm sugar
Peanut oil
Roasted rice powder (sold in small packets)
Sesame oil
Tamarind pulp or dried tamarind
Turmeric, ground
White rice

2

Hot and Sour Prawn Soup
Tom Yum Goong

It would be difficult to say which is the more popular soup of Thailand—this or Chicken and Coconut Soup with Galangal, Tom Kha Gai (see page 4). Even people who do not speak the Thai language know these by their Thai names. If this soup is one of your favourites, make a batch of Tom Yum Paste (see page 175) and have it ready in the fridge. Then a bowl of this soup is only minutes away—boil the water, dissolve the spicy paste and cook the prawns.

Serves 6

500 g (1 lb) raw prawns
1 tablespoon peanut oil
2 litres (4 pints/8 cups) water
1 teaspoon salt
2 stems lemongrass, white portion only, thinly sliced
6 slices fresh galangal
6 kaffir lime leaves, whole
3 fresh red chillies, sliced
2 teaspoons chopped garlic
2 tablespoons fish sauce
3 tablespoons lime juice
2 tablespoons chopped coriander leaves
4 spring onions, chopped
chopped red chilli (optional)

Shell the prawns, reserving the heads and shells. Dry the shells on kitchen paper.

Heat the oil in a saucepan and fry the shells and heads until they turn red. Add water, salt, lemongrass, galangal, lime leaves, chillies and garlic. Cover and simmer for 20 minutes, then strain and reserve the stock.

Devein the prawns, drop them into the stock and simmer for a few minutes until they are cooked. Add the fish sauce and lime juice to taste, remove from the heat at once and serve sprinkled with the coriander and spring onions and a little extra red chilli if desired.

3

Chicken and Coconut Soup with Galangal
Tom Kha Gai

Creamy and mild with plenty of aroma and flavour from the galangal, lime leaves, lemongrass and green chillies.

Serves 6

1 small roasting chicken
1 × 560 ml (19 fl oz) can coconut milk
6 slices fresh galangal
freshly ground black pepper
1 tablespoon chopped coriander roots
2 stems lemongrass, white portion only, thinly sliced
3 fresh green chillies, whole
1½ teaspoons salt
4 fresh or frozen kaffir lime leaves
1 tablespoon fish sauce
juice of 1–2 limes
chopped fresh coriander leaves

Cut the chicken into joints: divide the drumstick from the thigh, the wings from the breast, and cut the breast pieces in half. Chop the back into three pieces.

Put the chicken into a saucepan. Dilute 300 ml (10 fl oz) of the canned coconut milk with 500 ml (16 fl oz/2 cups) water and pour over the chicken. Add galangal, pepper, coriander roots, lemongrass, chillies, salt and lime leaves. Bring to a simmer over low heat and cook, uncovered, until the chicken is tender, stirring occasionally.

Add the remaining undiluted coconut milk and stir constantly until it reaches simmering point again. Remove from heat, stir in the fish sauce and lime juice and ladle into bowls. Sprinkle with chopped coriander and serve with steamed rice.

4

Pumpkin and Coconut Soup

I've taken a classic Thai recipe and modernised it, reducing the preparation time dramatically.

Serves 6

500 g (1 lb) ripe pumpkin
750 ml (24 fl oz/3 cups) water or chicken stock
2 tablespoons Tom Yum Paste (page 175) or Reuben Solomon's Singapore
    Laksa Paste
1 x 400 ml (13 fl oz) can coconut milk
fish sauce or salt
lime juice to taste
a few small basil leaves

Peel and dice the pumpkin, discarding any seeds.

Bring water or stock to the boil in a saucepan and stir in the paste. Add 100 ml (3½ fl oz) of the coconut milk and the diced pumpkin. Simmer until the pumpkin is tender.

Stir in the rest of the coconut milk and mash some of the pumpkin to give thickness to the soup. Taste and adjust the seasoning, if necessary, with a dash of fish sauce or salt, and a little lime juice. Ladle into bowls and scatter basil leaves over when serving.

Thai Fish Cakes
Tod Mun Pla

There are different versions of Thai fish cakes. The commonest fish cakes are fried, resulting in a bouncy, rubbery texture that some people accept but others dislike. My first experience with fish cakes was in an exclusive restaurant in Thailand where the chef was a minor princess who had learned her craft in a palace kitchen. The fish cakes she presented were exquisitely moulded in tiny fish shapes and steamed so their texture was tender, almost like a mousseline. Ever since, I have been spoiled for fried fish cakes. I realise that not everybody has a steamer or the space to accommodate one, so this recipe is adapted for use in an oven, thus resulting in a tender, moist fish cake. Readily available in kitchen shops are trays of non-stick patty cake tins, which are ideal for baking these fish cakes. The recipe may be doubled or trebled for parties and served as finger food. Make a day ahead, except for the garnish, cover with plastic and refrigerate until required.

Makes 12 small fish cakes

300 g (10 oz) skinless fillets of delicate white fish
2 teaspoons Red Curry Paste (page 173)
2 teaspoons fish sauce
½ teaspoon finely grated lime zest
a pinch of white pepper
125 ml (4 fl oz/½ cup) canned coconut milk
1 tablespoon finely chopped spring onions or chives
2 teaspoons rice flour
¼ teaspoon salt
thinly sliced red chillies
kaffir lime leaves, finely shredded

Preheat the oven to 200°C (400°F).

Remove any traces of skin and stray bones from the fish and dice the fillets. Mince finely in food processor for just a few seconds. Mix together the curry paste, fish sauce, lime zest, pepper and 2 tablespoons of the coconut milk and pour through the feed tube while processing the fish for a further 30 seconds. Scoop the fish mixture into a bowl and mix in the spring onions or chives. Divide into 12 even portions and with oiled palms roll each into a ball. Press flat and place in oiled patty pans.

Bake the fish cakes for 5–6 minutes. Do not overcook.

Combine the remaining coconut milk with the rice flour and salt in a small saucepan over low heat, stirring until the mixture boils and thickens. Spoon a little onto each fish cake, and decorate with a chilli slice and shreds of kaffir lime leaf or use a single leaf of fresh coriander or small-leaf basil.

Serve 2 fish cakes on a bed of soft lettuce as a first course.

6

Thai-style Dips and Crudites

A nice way to ring the changes on ever-popular raw vegetables with dips is to use a Thai dip. It livens up bland vegetables like you wouldn't believe. Here are recipes for two dips, one a vegetarian version.

Shrimp Dip (Nam Prik)
3 tablespoons small dried shrimp
1 clove garlic
2 shallots or small red onions
2 fresh red chillies
2 tablespoons lime juice
2 teaspoons palm sugar
2 tablespoons fish sauce
2 tablespoons water

Buy dried shrimp that are bright pink in colour and not too hard to the touch. Wash the dried shrimp and soak in a little warm water to cover for 10 minutes. Remove any sandy veins. Put the drained shrimp into a mortar and pound them with the garlic, shallots and chillies until mashed to a paste. Gradually stir in the lime juice, palm sugar, fish sauce and sufficient water to give a coating consistency.

Serve in a small bowl surrounded by sticks of raw cucumber, celery and carrots, or lightly cooked asparagus and green beans.

Eggplant Dip (Nam Prik Makua)
1 medium-sized eggplant, about 350 g (11 oz)
1 lime
3 small purple shallots, peeled
1 small clove garlic, crushed
½ teaspoon salt or to taste
1 teaspoon palm sugar
1 fresh red chilli, sliced

Bring a pan of lightly salted water to the boil. Peel and dice the eggplant and drop into the water. Boil until tender, about 8 minutes. Drain well.

Finely grate the lime zest and squeeze the juice.

Put the eggplant into a food processor or blender with the rest of the ingredients and blend at high speed to form a purée. Taste and add more lime juice, salt or sugar if necessary. Serve with vegetables for dipping.

Stir-fried Rice Noodles
Pad Thai

One of the most popular street-side snacks of Thailand, this dish of rice noodles is quickly stir-fried with seasonings, most of which are pantry basics.

Serves 2–4

200 g (7 oz) flat rice noodles, about 3mm (⅛ in wide)
3 tablespoons oil
6 large raw prawns, which have been shelled and deveined (optional)
salt and pepper
1 tablespoon chopped garlic
2 tablespoons sliced shallots
125 g (4 oz) fresh beansprouts, washed and drained
2 eggs, beaten
2 teaspoons sugar
2 tablespoons fish sauce or light soy sauce
3 tablespoons water
1 tablespoon lime or lemon juice
6 spring onions, cut into bite-sized lengths
1 small bunch garlic chives, chopped
3 tablespoons small dried shrimp, roughly pounded
2 tablespoons chopped pickled radish (optional)
1 tablespoon sweet chilli sauce
4 tablespoons roughly chopped roasted peanuts
1 teaspoon dried chilli flakes
roasted peanuts, extra
lime or lemon wedges for serving

Soak the rice noodles in hot (not boiling) water for 20 minutes while you prepare the other ingredients. Drain well before cooking.

Heat 1 tablespoon of the oil in a wok and stir-fry the raw prawns, if using, sprinkling salt to taste. Remove the prawns from the wok, add the remaining oil and fry the garlic and shallots over low heat making sure they don't burn. Add half the beansprouts and toss for a few seconds, then pour in the beaten eggs seasoned with salt and pepper.

Add the drained noodles and toss to mix, then add sugar, fish sauce, water and lemon juice, stirring until the sugar dissolves. Keep tossing until the noodles are cooked. Add the spring onions, garlic chives, dried shrimp, pickled radish, chilli sauce and roasted peanuts and toss for 1–2 minutes. Return the cooked prawns and heat through.

Serve hot, garnished with small piles of chilli flakes, extra roasted peanuts and the reserved beansprouts. The lemon or lime wedges are to be squeezed over individual servings as desired.

Crisp Rice Noodles
Mee Grob

Another noodle dish featuring many of the same flavours that go into Pad Thai (see page 8), but the texture is different because of the noodles used. These are the fine vermicelli, which are fried crisp and should be served soon after they are combined with the other ingredients. Mee grob works better as a taste teaser rather than a main dish.

Serves 4–6

125 g (4 oz) rice vermicelli
500 ml (16 fl oz/2 cups) oil for deep-frying
200 g (7 oz) firm bean curd, diced small
100 g (3½ oz) minced pork or chicken
100 g (3½ oz) chopped raw prawns
2 tablespoons white vinegar
2 tablespoons sugar
2 tablespoons fish sauce
2 eggs, beaten
1 whole bulb pickled garlic
1–2 finely sliced hot chillies
4 tablespoons chopped fresh coriander

Separate the rice vermicelli into small handfuls because it puffs and increases in size when it is fried. (It helps to first put the noodles into a large plastic bag and work inside the bag, otherwise bits of noodle will scatter over your kitchen floor.)

Heat the oil in a wok and when a haze rises from the surface, test the heat by frying a few strands of noodles, which should swell immediately. If not, wait until the oil heats up a bit more, then fry a handful at a time. The noodles should turn pale golden in a few seconds. Immediately lift out of the oil and drain on several sheets of absorbent paper. Leave to cool. Fry the diced bean curd until golden. Lift out on a slotted spoon and drain on absorbent paper.

Strain the oil into a heatproof bowl. (It may be re-used.) Return 2 tablespoons of oil to the wok and stir-fry the minced pork or chicken on high heat until the colour changes. Add the prawns and stir-fry for 1 minute longer.

Stir together the vinegar, sugar and fish sauce until the sugar dissolves.

Add the bean curd and the vinegar mixture to the wok. When the liquid boils, add the eggs and stir until the eggs set. Return the noodles to the wok and toss to combine. Transfer to a serving dish.

Slice the pickled garlic across the bulb and arrange around the noodles. Scatter sliced chillies and chopped coriander over and serve at once while the noodles are still crisp.

NOTE: Pickled garlic is sold in jars at Asian stores.

Stir-fried Bean Starch Noodles
Pad Woon Sen

While bean starch noodles may appear in cold dishes such as salads, they are also served hot and highly seasoned. This is one of the quickest ways to get a tasty meal on the table, relying on the jar of Red Curry Paste or Charmaine Solomon's Thai Red Curry Paste I always have in the refrigerator.

Serves 4

200 g (7 oz) bean starch noodles
100 g (3½ oz) cooked meat, e.g. barbecued pork, chicken or
      Chinese sausage (*lap cheong*)
2 tablespoons oil
2–3 tablespoons Red Curry Paste (see page 173) or
      Charmaine Solomon's Thai Red Curry Paste
100 g (3½ oz) small cooked prawns, peeled
6 spring onions, sliced
50 g (1½ oz) roasted peanuts, coarsely crushed
salt or fish sauce
a few sprigs of fresh coriander, chopped
lime or lemon wedges for serving

Soak the noodles in a bowl of hot water for 10 minutes. Drain. Depending on the thickness of the noodles, cook them in a pan of lightly salted boiling water for 3–4 minutes if using the fine bean threads, or 8 minutes for the 3 mm (⅛ in) wide noodles. Drain well.

Slice the meat you are using. If using Chinese sausage, steam over boiling water for 5–8 minutes until swollen and soft. Slice diagonally.

Heat the oil in a wok. On medium heat fry the curry paste, stirring, for 1 minute. Add the noodles and toss until the curry paste is evenly distributed over the noodles. Toss in the cooked meat and prawns, spring onions and half the peanuts. Stir-fry until the noodles are well mixed. Taste and adjust the seasoning, adding a little salt or fish sauce if required. Serve sprinkled with the remaining peanuts and the coriander. Lime or lemon wedges may be offered for squeezing over individual servings.

NOTE: I advise buying bean starch noodles in plastic net bags containing 8 small bundles of 50 g (1½ oz) each. If purchased in 500 g (1 lb) hanks, they are fiddly to separate and have to be cut with scissors.

Chilli Fried Rice
Khao Pad Prik

Leftover rice is a very useful thing to have in the refrigerator—it makes the beginnings of a one-dish meal such as fried rice. If you don't have any rice ready, you will need the first paragraph of the recipe, otherwise start at the second step.

Serves 4

2 cups rice
750 ml (24 fl oz/3 cups) water
3 tablespoons vegetable oil
3 tablespoons Red Curry Paste (see page 173) or
        Charmaine Solomon's Thai Red Curry Paste
100 g (3 ½ oz) pork, finely diced or minced
250 g (8 oz) small raw prawns, shelled and deveined, or 2 tablespoons dried
        shrimp, soaked and drained
2 eggs, beaten
salt and pepper
1 tablespoon fish sauce
1 cup chopped spring onions
1 red chilli, sliced
1 green chilli, sliced
½ cup chopped fresh coriander

Wash the rice and drain well. Bring the rice and water to the boil in a heavy saucepan with a well-fitting lid. Turn the heat to very low and cook for 15 minutes without lifting lid. Remove from the heat and leave to stand for a further 10 minutes. Turn the rice onto a large baking dish or tray and leave to cool. If possible, refrigerate overnight. You should have 4 cups of cold rice.

If you have a rice cooker, combine the rice and water, cook and set aside to cool.

Heat the oil in a wok and fry the curry paste on medium heat, stirring, for 1 minute. Add the pork and stir-fry until cooked. If you are only able to buy large prawns, cut them in half and add to the wok, frying for a few minutes until they are cooked. Add dried shrimp if using.

Add the rice, toss and mix until the grains are coated with the spice mixture and heated through. Push the rice to the edge of the wok, leaving a space in the centre, and pour in the beaten eggs seasoned with salt and pepper. Stir until they start to set. Mix with the rice and toss over high heat until the eggs are cooked.

Sprinkle with fish sauce. Scatter spring onions and chillies over and toss for a further minute. Serve garnished with fresh coriander.

12

Thai Seafood Salad

Because their red stripes are so pretty, I am specifying tiger prawns to contrast with the snowy whiteness of the squid.

Serves 4

300 g (10 oz) tiger prawns
300 g (10 oz) squid tubes
4 fresh kaffir lime leaves
2 stems lemongrass
1 teaspoon salt
2 tablespoons fish sauce
3 tablespoons lime juice
2 teaspoons palm sugar
1 teaspoon crushed garlic
1 teaspoon finely chopped tender ginger
4 tablespoons finely sliced spring onions
6 sprigs fresh mint
3 sprigs fresh coriander
3 fresh red chillies, finely sliced
soft lettuce such as oak leaf
lime wedges for serving

Shell the prawns, leaving the tails on. Slit the curve of the back and remove the tract.

Cut the squid tubes open and rinse well. Score the inner surface with diagonal cuts, holding the knife at a 45-degree angle. Cut into bite-sized pieces about 5 cm (2 in) square.

Put the lime leaves, lemongrass and salt into a saucepan with about 750 ml (24 fl oz/3 cups) water and bring to a boil. Simmer for 5 minutes to flavour the water. Drop in the squid and as soon as the pieces curl and become white and opaque, lift them out with a slotted spoon. This should take less than a minute. Do not overcook or the squid will toughen. Add the prawns to the same water and cook only until they become opaque and the stripes are red. Lift out and combine with the squid in a bowl.

Combine the fish sauce, lime juice, palm sugar, garlic and ginger. Toss the seafood in the dressing. Add the spring onions, mint, coriander and chillies. Toss lightly, arrange on the lettuce leaves and serve at room temperature. Garnish each serving with a wedge of lime.

13

Thai Green Curry of Fish

Serves 4

500 g (1 lb) fillets of boneless white fish such as ling or snapper
1 x 400 ml (13 fl oz) can coconut milk
3 tablespoons Green Curry Paste (see page 174) or
      Charmaine Solomon's Thai Green Curry Paste
fresh coriander or Thai basil leaves

Wipe the fish fillets with a damp paper towel in case there are stray scales on them. Cut into serving size pieces.

   Shake the can of coconut milk vigorously before opening it. In a wok heat half the coconut milk until bubbling. Stir in the curry paste and simmer for 5 minutes. Add remaining milk, slide in the pieces of fish and spoon the sauce over. Cook uncovered for just long enough to cook the fish—the exact time will depend on the thickness of the fillets. Turn off the heat and stir in the fresh herbs, then spoon into a dish and serve with steamed jasmine rice.

Thai Red Curry of Prawns

Cooks in Thailand usually leave the shells on the prawns, and there is no denying that they do have a more intense flavour. If you are worried things could get messy at the table, split the shell down the back and remove the vein before cooking. Then it is a simple matter for diners to extract the meat from the shell with spoon and fork.

Serves 6

24 large raw prawns or 30 medium-sized raw prawns
1 × 400 ml (13 fl oz) can coconut milk
3 tablespoons Red Curry Paste (see page 173) or
      Charmaine Solomon's Thai Red Curry Paste
4 fresh kaffir lime leaves
finely grated zest of 1 kaffir lime
1–2 tablespoons fish sauce
1 teaspoon palm sugar (optional)

Use kitchen scissors to cut open the prawn shell down the curve of the back. With a sharp knife slit prawn just enough to expose the sandy intestinal tract and lift it out.

In a wok or heavy pan heat half the coconut milk until bubbling. Stir in the curry paste and cook, stirring, until it is thick and fragrant. Stir in the rest of the coconut milk, lime leaves and zest, fish sauce and palm sugar. Bring to a simmer.

Add the prawns and, if they are not submerged, top up the sauce by adding a little water. Simmer uncovered, stirring occasionally, until the prawns are cooked and the sauce slightly reduced and thick. This may take 15 minutes, depending on the size of the prawns. Serve with steamed rice.

Chicken in Pandan Leaves

Pandan leaves (long, flat and strap-like) are used in many ways in Asian cooking. Until recently they were only exported in dried form. A couple of strips boiled with rice give a good flavour. They are also simmered in curries.

Fresh pandan leaves are sold in Asian shops and it is worth looking for them. They are pounded to a paste to flavour and colour cakes and puddings. In Thailand they are used to fashion tiny cases for sweets, which not only look dainty but also impart their delicate flavour. This recipe is a perfect example of how they wrap and flavour at the same time.

Serves 4

500 g (1 lb) chicken thigh fillets
1–2 tablespoons Pepper, Garlic and Coriander Paste (see page 172) or
        Charmaine Solomon's Thai Barbecue Marinade
1 teaspoon finely grated ginger
1 tablespoon finely chopped shallots
2 tablespoons fish sauce
2 tablespoons coconut milk
1 teaspoon palm sugar or brown sugar
pandan leaves, fresh or frozen (dried are not suitable)

Trim any excess fat from the chicken and cut the meat into bite-sized pieces. Combine all the remaining ingredients (except the pandan leaves) and mix well with the chicken. Cover and leave to marinate for 30 minutes or longer.

If using frozen pandan leaves, leave at room temperature to thaw and become flexible. Place 2 pieces of chicken on each strip of pandan leaf which should be cut just long enough to completely wrap the chicken. Fasten with toothpicks.

When the little parcels are all made cook them over glowing coals on a barbecue or under a preheated griller, about a handspan from the source of heat. Turn them after 4 minutes and cook for a further 4 minutes. Serve straight away. Diners need to unwrap the parcels before eating.

Barbecued Garlic Chicken

Despite its simplicity this has proved to be one of the most popular Thai recipes. Chicken is marinated in a mixture of garlic, pepper and coriander, then barbecued. A roasting chicken may be used or, if it is more convenient, use thigh cutlets or boned half-breasts with the skin left on.

Serves 6

1.5 kg (3 lb) roasting chicken or 6 chicken thigh or breast fillets
3 tablespoons Pepper, Garlic and Coriander Paste (see page 172) or
     Charmaine Solomon's Thai Barbecue Marinade

Cut the chicken in half lengthways. Make shallow slits in the breast and thigh. Rub the marinade into the chicken on all sides, cover with plastic wrap and refrigerate overnight or leave at room temperature for at least 1 hour.

    Barbecue over glowing coals about 15 cm (6 in) from heat. Turn with tongs every 5 minutes until the chicken is no longer pink in the middle and the skin is nicely browned and crisp. Serve with a salad of cucumber slices, spring onions and tomatoes.

Chiang Mai Salad
Larb

This salad has such a following among westerners because its flavours are so refreshing. The tang of lime juice, the fragrance of fresh herbs and the nutty aroma of roasted rice make it unlike any other salad. It can be based on beef, chicken or venison.

Serves 4

2 tablespoons oil
2 tablespoons Pepper, Garlic and Coriander Paste (see page 172) or
     Charmaine Solomon's Thai Barbecue Marinade
500 g (1 lb) premium minced beef, chicken or venison
3 fresh kaffir lime leaves
3 tablespoons roasted rice powder
2 tablespoons fish sauce
3 tablespoons lime juice
1 teaspoon sugar
2 stems lemongrass, white portion only, finely sliced
1 large red onion, finely sliced
6 spring onions , finely chopped
2 fresh red chillies, sliced (optional)
6 sprigs fresh mint
6 sprigs fresh coriander
a few leaves of Vietnamese mint (*rau ram*)
lettuce leaves

Heat the oil in a wok or frying pan and gently fry the paste for a minute or until fragrant. Add the meat and stir-fry on medium heat until all pinkness has gone. Cover and simmer for 5 minutes, then turn into a bowl and leave to cool.

Finely shred the kaffir lime leaves into thread-like strips, discarding the tough mid-rib.

Sprinkle roasted rice powder over the beef. Stir together the fish sauce, lime juice and sugar until the sugar dissolves. Pour over the meat and mix well, adding all the other ingredients except the lettuce. Chop the fresh herbs just before adding so they don't lose their colour. Pile meat mixture on lettuce leaves and serve.

NOTE: Roasted rice may be purchased in small packets in Asian stores. If you cannot find it, make it at home by roasting ½ cup raw rice grains over low heat in a heavy pan, stirring constantly, until they are golden brown. This takes about 10 minutes. Grind to powder in a blender and store in an airtight jar.

19

Masaman Curry of Beef

Masaman is the Thai term for Muslim, and this is one of the most popular curries of Thailand. The dish is a complex blend of traditional flavours and the fragrant spices of India introduced by Muslim traders. It is rather a sweet curry.

Serves 6–8

750 g (1½ lb) round steak or other stewing beef
1 teaspoon salt
5 green cardamom pods, bruised
300 ml (10 fl oz) water
1 × 560 ml (19 fl oz) can coconut milk
4 tablespoons Masaman Curry Paste (see page 176) or
        Charmaine Solomon's Thai Masaman Curry Paste
8 small new potatoes, whole
4 tablespoons roasted peanuts
1 tablespoon fish sauce
3 tablespoons lime juice
2 teaspoons palm sugar
30 basil leaves

Cut the beef into cubes and put into a pan with the salt, cardamom pods, water and 300 ml (10 fl oz) coconut milk. Bring to the boil and simmer, uncovered, until the beef is half-cooked. Take off the heat and allow to cool in the liquid. Reserve the cooking liquid.

In a separate pan, heat the remaining coconut milk until bubbling, stir in the curry paste and fry until fragrant. Stir in the potatoes, peanuts, beef and 250 ml (8 fl oz/1 cup) of the cooking liquid. Simmer until tender, adding some of the stock if it becomes too dry.

Stir in the fish sauce, lime juice and palm sugar. Just before serving, add the basil leaves. Serve with steamed rice.

Thai Eggplant Curry

In Thailand, many kinds of eggplant are used and in Australia we are also being offered a variety. The most common kind, however, are large purple eggplants, and they are superb in this dish, though you may use other types if available.

Serves 4

500 g (1 lb) eggplant
oil for deep-frying
2 tablespoons Pepper, Garlic and Coriander Paste (see page 172) or
     Green Curry Paste (see page 174)
250 ml (8 fl oz/1 cup) canned coconut milk
2 tablespoons fish sauce
1 tablespoon palm sugar
chopped fresh coriander

Wash and dry eggplant but do not peel. If using slender eggplant, cut into short slices crossways. Cut large eggplant into large cubes. Deep-fry a few at a time in hot oil until well browned. Lift out on a slotted spoon and drain on absorbent paper.

Heat 1 tablespoon of oil and on low heat fry the paste for 1–2 minutes, stirring. Add the coconut milk, diluted with an equal amount of water. Bring to the boil. Stir in the fish sauce and palm sugar and simmer for 5 minutes, then add the eggplant and simmer for 10 minutes or until the eggplant is tender. Sprinkle with chopped coriander and serve with steamed rice.

21

Burmese Fish Soup with Noodles
Moh Hin Gha

A soup just as central to Burmese cuisine as Tom Yum Goong (see page 3) and Tom Kha Gai (see page 4) are to Thai cuisine. This one-dish meal is considered by many to be the national dish of Burma. One of the ingredients, the heart of a banana tree, used to be available only to those who grow bananas, but now many Asian food stores sell sections of fresh banana heart. To use, discard the outer layers and cut the tender inner portion into thin slices crossways. Soak the slices in a large bowl of salted water for several hours. The sticky juice forms hair-like threads which should be pulled away and discarded. If this is not practical for you, use thin slices of canned bamboo shoot as a substitute.

Serves 6–8

500 g (1 lb) fillets of strong-flavoured fish or 2 cans herrings in
    tomato sauce
salt
4 large onions, roughly chopped
6 cloves garlic
1 tablespoon chopped ginger
1 teaspoon ground turmeric
½–1 teaspoon chilli powder
2 fresh red chillies, seeded and chopped
2 tablespoons dark sesame oil
4 tablespoons peanut oil
2 × 400 ml (13 fl oz) cans coconut milk
250 g (8 oz) banana heart or bamboo shoots, sliced
1 teaspoon dried shrimp paste
1 tablespoon fish sauce
3 tablespoons chickpea flour
lemon juice to taste
salt to taste
500 g (1 lb) rice vermicelli
accompaniments as desired

If using fresh fish fillets, simmer in lightly salted water for 5 minutes and reserve the fish stock for adding to the soup later.

In a food processor or blender, purée the onions, garlic, ginger, turmeric, chilli powder and chillies.

Heat the sesame and peanut oils in a large saucepan and add the purée when it is very hot. Cover the pan, reduce the heat and fry the purée over very low heat for at least 20 minutes, stirring frequently. If it starts to stick, add a little water from time to time.

When the water content of the onions has evaporated the mixture should be a reddish brown and oil should separate around the edges. This is the important technique that results in the mellow flavour typical of Burmese food. Add 1 can coconut milk diluted with 2 cans of water, and the drained banana heart or bamboo shoots. Bring to the boil, turn the heat to low and simmer until the banana heart is tender.

Dissolve the dried shrimp paste in the fish sauce and add to the pan. Mix the chickpea flour with a little cold water until smooth and stir into the soup. Keep stirring until it comes to the boil and cook for 5 minutes.

Add the remaining can of coconut milk, stirring as it comes to a simmer. Add flaked fish fillets and fish stock or canned fish together with the sauce in the cans. Taste the soup and adjust the seasoning with lemon juice and salt.

Cook the rice vermicelli in lightly salted boiling water for 2 minutes or until just tender. Drain well and serve in a bowl alongside the soup. To eat, place the noodles in bowls and ladle over the piping hot soup. Diners can add accompaniments of their choice, which may be any or all of the following:

finely sliced spring onions
chopped fresh coriander
finely sliced white onion
roasted chickpeas, finely ground in a blender
fried onion flakes
crisp-fried garlic
lime or lemon wedges
dried chillies, fried in oil for 3–4 seconds
chilli powder

NOTE: Roasted chickpeas may be purchased from Greek delicatessens.

Burmese Chicken Curry with Noodles
Panthé Kaukswé

In Burmese cuisine, it is quite in order for guests to adjust the flavour of their food to taste, say, by squeezing over a little lemon juice if they want more piquancy, adding a sprinkling of chilli powder for heat, a scattering of fresh coriander and spring onions or some slices of fried garlic.

This mild curry with lots of soupy gravy is another of the one-course meals typical of Burmese cooking.

Serves 6–8

2 kg (4 lb) chicken joints
8 cloves garlic, chopped
4 medium-sized onions, chopped
1 tablespoon chopped ginger
1 teaspoon dried shrimp paste
2 tablespoons peanut oil
2 tablespoons dark sesame oil
1–2 teaspoons chilli powder
2 teaspoons salt or to taste
1 × 560 ml (19 fl oz) can coconut milk
2 tablespoons chickpea flour
500 g (1 lb) fine egg noodles or bean thread vermicelli
accompaniments as for Moh Hin Gha (see page 22)

Thighs, drumsticks and wings are the best pieces to use as they stand up to long cooking better than delicate breast meat. If jointing a whole chicken, add the breast pieces after the other joints are almost tender.

Purée the garlic, onions, ginger and dried shrimp paste in a blender. Heat the oils in a heavy pan and fry the blended ingredients, stirring, for 10 minutes. Add the chicken and continue to fry, stirring constantly. Add chilli powder, salt and half the coconut milk diluted with an equal amount of water. Simmer uncovered until the chicken is tender.

Stir in the remaining coconut milk and heat gently, stirring constantly. Mix the chickpea flour with a little cold water to form a smooth cream. Add to the pan and cook for a further 5 minutes. There will be lots of sauce.

Close to serving time, cook the noodles in a large saucepan of salted boiling water until just tender. Pour cold water into the pan to stop noodles cooking, and drain in a colander.

Serve the noodles and curry in separate bowls, and offer accompaniments for diners to choose from.

24

Burmese Curry of Beef with Potatoes
Amétha Net Aloo Hin

Not just a way of stretching a meal to feed more people, the effect of vegetables cooked in spices is very pleasing. If preferred, diced pumpkin may be substituted for potatoes.

Serves 6–8

3 large onions, cut into eighths
5 large cloves garlic, roughly chopped
2 teaspoons finely grated fresh ginger
4 tablespoons peanut oil
2 tablespoons dark sesame oil
1 teaspoon ground turmeric
1 teaspoon chilli powder
1 teaspoon ground cumin
1 teaspoon ground coriander
750 g (1½ lb) beef round, chuck or other stewing steak,
    cut into 2.5 cm (1 in) cubes
1½ teaspoons salt or to taste
500 ml (16 fl oz/2 cups) hot water
500 g (1 lb) potatoes, peeled and quartered

Put the onions, garlic and ginger into food processor and process until the onions are finely chopped.

In a heavy-based saucepan heat both oils and when very hot add the onion mixture. Turn the heat to low and place a lid on the pan. Add the ground spices and cook, stirring frequently, until the mixture smells fragrant. It may be necessary to add a little water from time to time to prevent the mixture from sticking to the base of the pan. When the oil separates from the mass and shows around the edges and on top, add the meat and fry, stirring to coat with the spice and onion mixture. Add salt and half the water, cover the pan and cook until the beef is half-done. Add the potatoes and remaining hot water and cook until the vegetables are tender.

Serve with freshly cooked white rice and a green vegetable such as Greens with Shrimp Paste (see page 65) or Thai Eggplant Curry (see page 21).

Burmese Pork Curry
Wethani Kyet

This delicious curry no doubt owes much to the large quantity of garlic and ginger used, but also to the long, slow cooking that develops the unique flavour.

Serves 6–8

3 large onions, roughly chopped
20 cloves garlic, peeled
1 cup peeled, sliced ginger
1.5 kg (3 lb) pork loin or thick leg chops, cut into large cubes
2 teaspoons salt
2 tablespoons vinegar
1–2 teaspoons chilli powder
8 tablespoons peanut oil
4 tablespoons dark sesame oil
1 teaspoon ground turmeric

Put the onions, garlic and ginger into food processor or blender and process until finely chopped. Set a strainer over a saucepan and turn the chopped mixture into it, pressing out as much liquid as possible. Reserve the solids left in the strainer.

To the liquid in the pan, add the pork, salt, vinegar, chilli powder and 4 tablespoons of the peanut oil. Bring to the boil, cover and simmer over low heat for $1\frac{1}{2}$ hours or until the pork is tender. If necessary, top up with a little hot water.

In another heavy saucepan heat the remaining peanut oil and sesame oil. When very hot, add the onion purée. Cook over low heat, stirring frequently, until the mixture turns a rich reddish brown. From time to time add 1–2 tablespoons water to prevent the mixture from sticking to the pan or burning. Spoon off some of the oil that rises to the top of the pork mixture and add it to the cooking onions with the turmeric.

When the oil separates from the pork add the onion mixture to the pan and cook uncovered over medium heat until the oil separates again. The pork should be stirred frequently when it reaches the stage where the liquid is almost evaporated or it could stick to the base of the pan and scorch. Serve with steamed rice and vegetable accompaniments.

Vietnamese Fried Spring Rolls
Cha Gio

Makes 24

1 small (50 g/1½ oz) bundle bean thread vermicelli
3 golden shallots, finely chopped
3 spring onions, finely chopped
250 g (8 oz) minced pork or beef
250 g (8 oz) raw prawns, chopped
100 g (3½ oz) cooked crab meat
1 tablespoon fish sauce
½ teaspoon salt
½ teaspoon sugar
¼ teaspoon ground black pepper
24 sheets spring roll wrappers or Vietnamese rice paper rounds
oil for deep-frying
Nuoc Cham (see page 37)

Remove the threads tying the bundle of vermicelli, place vermicelli in a bowl and pour boiling water over. Soak for 15 minutes, then drain and cut the vermicelli into short lengths. Combine with the shallots, spring onions, pork, prawns, crab meat, fish sauce, salt, sugar and pepper.

If using spring roll wrappers, cut the sheets in half. Return to the plastic packet or cover the wrappers with a tea towel or they will dry out and be difficult to use. Shape 2 teaspoons of filling into a neat roll and place on one end of the wrapper. Fold in the ends and roll up so the filling is completely enclosed.

If using rice paper circles or triangles, dip each one quickly in tepid water for a few seconds to make them pliable, or brush the paper with a pastry brush dipped in water. Lay them on a working surface. Take 2 teaspoons of filling and shape into a neat roll. Place near one end of the circle, bring in the sides to cover the filling and roll up to enclose. Do not roll too tightly or the rolls may split during frying. Lay the rolls on sheets of absorbent kitchen paper and let them dry out slightly before frying. When all are made, deep-fry a few at a time in hot oil over medium heat until crisp and golden. Do not have the heat too high or they will brown before the filling cooks through. Drain on absorbent kitchen paper.

Serve with soft lettuce leaves (oak leaf lettuce is suitable) and a selection of fresh herbs such as mint, coriander, Vietnamese mint (*rau ram*), slender cucumber spears and fresh beansprouts. Each roll is wrapped in a lettuce leaf with a cucumber spear and choice of herbs, then dipped in Nuoc Cham and eaten.

Fresh Rice Paper Rolls

A traditional Vietnamese snack, these are becoming very popular with health-conscious Westerners as a low-fat version of fried spring rolls. The filling is based on cooked ingredients, but the fresh herbs and dipping sauce are the same.

Makes 8–10

Filling
250 g (8 oz) small raw prawns in their shells
125 ml (4 fl oz/½ cup) water
1 tablespoon white vinegar
½ teaspoon salt
250 g (8 oz) pork fillet
2 tablespoons oil
2 cloves garlic, finely chopped
1 tablespoon fish sauce
1 teaspoon sugar

a few garlic chives
coriander sprigs
mint or Vietnamese mint (*rau ram*)
lettuce leaf
rice paper rounds
lettuce leaves
Nuoc Cham (see page 37)

To make the Filling, cook the prawns in a shallow pan with the water, vinegar and salt. Cool and peel.

Brown the pork fillet in the oil in another pan. Add the garlic and fry for 30 seconds, then add the liquid the prawns were cooked in, the fish sauce and sugar. Cover and cook for 10 minutes or until the pork is tender and the liquid is almost completely reduced. Cool and cut the pork into fine slices.

Arrange the pork, prawns, garlic chives, coriander and mint on a platter.

To eat, dip the dried rice paper rounds in tepid water for a few seconds until pliable. Fill each with prawns, pork, 1–2 garlic chives, a sprig of coriander and mint, then roll up. Wrap in a lettuce leaf and dip in Nuoc Cham.

Note: If liked, 100 g (3½ oz) rice vermicelli, cooked and drained, may be placed on the platter with pork and prawns. A small amount is added to the filling before rolling.

29

Vietnamese Sandwiches

The French influence is evident in the wonderful baguette sandwiches on sale in many Vietnamese hot bread shops. Try them if you come across a sandwich or cake shop. On the one side are the intricately colourful cakes, and one counter is often dedicated to sandwiches which are made to order. They aren't called sandwiches, though, but pork rolls.

A diagonal cut is deftly made in the crusty baguette and a smear of liver pâté applied on the bottom half. Butter is spread on the other half. Two or three very thin slices of white pork roll are laid on the pâté, then a similar amount of red pork roll and finally a thin slice of rolled roast pork with a brilliant red rind. A sprig of coriander, a length of spring onion and a spear of seedless cucumber are added, and finally about a tablespoon of finely shredded carrot which is doused with a squirt of soy sauce. (A Japanese grater is invaluable for shredding hard vegetables into thread-like strips.) You will be asked whether you wish sliced chillies to be added. They are large and red, but every bit as hot as the tiny bird's eye chillies which have earned such a reputation. In moderation, they add anticipation and excitement.

Never had such a sandwich graced the gambling rooms where the Earl of Sandwich gave his name to the hand-held snack of meat and bread. It is possible to buy pork rolls from the refrigerator section of any Vietnamese store if you wish to assemble your own baguettes à la Vietnam.

Shrimp on Sugar Cane Sticks

Fresh sugar cane is sold in some Asian shops, and if you find some, it is worth trying this delectable snack. The cane must be skinned with a sharp knife, cut into short lengths, then split into thin spears. Canned sugar cane may be used for the skewers. Each length of sugar cane should be split lengthways into 4–6 spears and patted dry.

Serves 6–8

500 g (1 lb) raw prawns
1 tablespoon oil
1 tablespoon fish sauce
1 egg white
60 g (2 oz) boiled pork fat, finely diced
½ teaspoon salt
a pinch of white pepper
1 teaspoon sugar
lengths of peeled sugar cane

Shell the prawns, slit along the curve and remove the sandy vein. Rinse the prawns in cold water and drain on absorbent paper. Chop very finely or purée in food processor, adding oil, fish sauce and egg white. When it is a soft paste remove from the processor and mix in the diced pork fat, salt, pepper and sugar. Mould heaped tablespoons of the mixture on sugar cane sticks.

Cook the sugar cane sticks over glowing coals on a barbecue or under a preheated griller.

Serve with soft lettuce leaves and rounds of moistened rice paper for wrapping, and sprigs of fresh mint and coriander and other fresh greens such as Vietnamese mint (*rau ram*).

Chicken with Bean Thread Vermicelli

A simply made Vietnamese dish.

Serves 4–5

150 g (5 oz) bean thread vermicelli
1 tablespoon oil
500 g (1 lb) chicken thigh or drumstick fillets, cut into bite-sized pieces
3 spring onions, thinly sliced
2 tablespoons fish sauce
¼ teaspoon ground black pepper
125 ml (4 fl oz/½ cup) water
2 firm ripe tomatoes, sliced
2 small white onions, sliced
1 teaspoon sugar
1 tablespoon vinegar
salt and pepper

Put the noodles into a bowl and pour over sufficient boiling water to cover. Leave to soak for 10 minutes. Drain and cut the noodles into short lengths.

Heat a wok, add the oil and stir-fry the chicken until it changes colour. Add the noodles and spring onions and toss for a further minute or two. Add fish sauce, pepper and water and simmer for 5 minutes.

Make a side salad by combining the tomatoes and onions with the sugar, vinegar, salt and pepper.

Serve the chicken hot with the side salad.

Chicken and Cabbage Salad

A friend who lived in Vietnam gave me this recipe. It is the most refreshing salad and we make it often for summer lunches.

Serves 6

500 g (1 lb) chicken thigh fillets
salt and pepper
1 small white Chinese cabbage
2 large red onions or 8 shallots, sliced
1 teaspoon salt
3 tablespoons sugar
3 tablespoons fish sauce
juice of 2 limes
1 tablespoon white vinegar
2 handfuls chopped mint or Vietnamese mint (*rau ram*)
2 handfuls chopped coriander leaves

Trim the chicken fillets of any fat and place in a saucepan with just enough water to cover. Add ½ teaspoon salt and a sprinkling of pepper. Bring to a slow simmer. Cover the pan and cook until the chicken is done, about 10 minutes. Let the chicken cool in the liquid.

Remove any discoloured or damaged outer leaves of the cabbage. Cut the cabbage into quarters lengthways, wash in cold water, shake off as much water as possible and shred very finely, crossways. Put the cabbage into a bowl, cover and chill.

Put the onions into a bowl, sprinkle with the salt and work the salt into the onions with your fingers. Leave for 30 minutes, rinse in cold water and squeeze out as much moisture as possible. This reduces the pungent flavour. Mix in half the sugar.

Combine the remaining sugar with the fish sauce, lime juice and vinegar.

Slice the cooled chicken thinly. Shortly before serving, combine the chicken, cabbage and onion with the dressing. Toss with mint and coriander.

33

Beef and Rice Noodle Soup
Pho

Here is the national dish of Vietnam, served and eaten at any time from breakfast to supper, in fancy restaurants or little take-away places, as well as in homes. The basis is a strong, well-flavoured beef stock simmered for hours.

Serves 8

Stock
1 kg (2 lb) shin beef
2 kg (4 lb) beef bones (not shin bones)
1 teaspoon whole black peppercorns
3 whole star anise
5 cardamom pods
6 whole cloves
1 cinnamon quill
1 onion, peeled and left whole
2 sprigs celery leaves
1 knob ginger, sliced
2 tablespoons fish sauce

500 g (1 lb) fresh rice noodles
250 g (8 oz) fresh mung beansprouts
1 white onion, thinly sliced
300 g (10 oz) beef fillet, thinly sliced
fresh mint, chopped
coriander, chopped
sliced chillies
lime wedges and fish sauce to taste

To make the Stock, in a large saucepan put the beef, bones, whole spices, onion, celery leaves, ginger and fish sauce. Add cold water to completely cover and bring to the boil, skimming the surface of froth several times. Turn the heat to very low, cover the pan and simmer for 5–6 hours, but remove the beef after 2 hours or when it has become tender. Strain the stock and add salt to taste. The stock may be made ahead and frozen, and reheated to boiling point when required.

To serve, pour boiling water over the rice noodles, drain and put a serve of noodles in each bowl with a handful of beansprouts. Scatter the onion slices over the noodles.

Bring the stock to the boil.

Put slices of beef into a large ladle and dip into the boiling stock. When the beef is pale pink, ladle over the noodles together with some stock. Serve at once, letting each person add fresh herbs and chillies to taste. Lime wedges and fish sauce are placed on the table and may be used to correct the seasoning.

Beef with Crushed Sesame Seeds and Bamboo Shoots

It is not advisable to double this recipe—better to cook it in two lots if serving more than four people.

Serves 4 with rice

4 tablespoons sesame seeds
3 tablespoons peanut oil
400 g (14 oz) lean fillet or rump steak, thinly sliced
1 piece canned winter bamboo shoot, drained and sliced
6 spring onions, cut into bite-sized pieces
1 teaspoon crushed garlic
2 tablespoons fish sauce

Toast the sesame seeds in a dry frying pan or wok, stirring constantly so they brown evenly. Turn out onto a plate to cool, then crush with a mortar and pestle or in a blender.

Heat a wok, add 2 tablespoons of the oil and when very hot stir-fry the beef quickly for 1 minute. Remove from the wok. Add the remaining tablespoon of oil and fry the bamboo shoot and spring onions for 2 minutes, then add the garlic and stir for 1 minute. Add the fish sauce, return the beef to the wok and stir-fry for a minute longer. Add the sesame seeds and mix well. Serve hot with rice.

Vietnamese Dipping Sauce
Nuoc Cham

There are many dipping sauces served with Vietnamese food. This is
a favourite, and is always used with spring rolls.

Makes 180 ml (6 fl oz/¾ cup)

1–2 hot red chillies
1–2 cloves garlic
1 teaspoon sugar
2 tablespoons lime juice
3 tablespoons fish sauce
1 tablespoon mild vinegar
3 tablespoons water

Remove the stems and seeds of chillies and chop the chillies very finely.
I advise wearing disposable gloves for this task.

 Smash the cloves of garlic against a wooden board with the flat of a knife
and lift off the skins. Sprinkle with sugar and work into a fine purée with the
knife blade. Combine all the ingredients in a bowl. Some versions add a little
finely shredded carrot.

Indonesia, Malaysia and Singapore

THE CULINARY BOUNDARIES between these countries are by no means clearly defined. What you may have tasted in one country is almost certain to be duplicated in the others. Who can say that satays, those tempting morsels of beef, chicken or pork threaded on bamboo skewers and cooked over charcoal fires, belong exclusively to Indonesia or Malaysia or Singapore? The same applies to the myriad noodle and rice dishes which form the basis of these cuisines; and some of the curries and accompaniments such as sambals, those explosive little vehicles for hot chillies, are as much at home in one country as another.

While much of the population of this melting pot is Muslim and their dishes would never feature pork, where the Chinese influence is predominant there will be recipes based on pork, yet using the spices of Malaysia as in the Nonya cooking of Singapore. Nonyas, (also known as Straits-born Chinese) are the descendants of Chinese immigrants and Malay locals. Intermarriage between the two races has created a most surprising and spicy cuisine.

Singapore is the most cosmopolitan city I have ever visited, and the variety of cuisines reflects the number of different ethnic groups who have settled there and made this small island a paradise for gourmets and gourmands. Most produce in Singapore is imported, not only from near neighbours Malaysia, Indonesia and Thailand who have more land to cultivate, but also from far away countries which offer fruits and vegetables grown in cooler climes. Air freight makes all things possible, so in this bustling, prosperous, tropical city, one can enjoy stone fruit, berries, cherries, apples, pears and grapes as well as mangosteens, durians, rambutans,

39

longans, mangoes and starfruit which are more at home in this part of the world. Leafy vegetables are grown by a small number of farmers, some of whom use hydroponic methods to grow vegetables in multi-storey factories.

Fish is a very important and popular item in Singapore, and both freshwater fish and seafood are farmed.

Malaysia also has a number of different ethnic groups such as Malays, Chinese and Indians, each with their own food styles. In some areas such as Malacca, the food has been powerfully influenced by the colonising Portuguese, yet spicier than the original, having in turn been given more than a passing brush with local flavours.

Indonesia, straddling the equator with its 18,000 islands (give or take a few) has the kind of steamy climate which requires highly spiced foods to tempt heat-jaded appetites.

To cover the cuisines of these countries you will need, in your pantry, a mixture of Chinese seasonings and sauces, plus Malaysian and Indonesian spices. In addition, purchase as needed fresh lemon grass, pandan leaves, chillies, and curry leaves. Hard tofu (bean curd) is sold in the refrigerator section of Asian stores. Years ago, when I wrote my first books, canned coconut milk was a thing of the future and when it first arrived on the market the quality was not great. Now, however, there are numerous satisfactory brands available. It is a perishable ingredient, so after opening a can and using the amount needed, pour the rest into an ice cube tray and freeze it. Store in freezer containers and use as required.

RECOMMENDED PANTRY

Bean sauce
Black beans, salted
Candle (*kemiri*) nuts
Chilli powder
Chilli sauce
Coconut milk, canned
Coconut, desiccated
Coriander, ground
Cumin, ground
Dried mushrooms and
     wood fungus
Dried shrimp paste (*blacan*)
Fennel, ground

Five-spice powder
Noodles and vermicelli of
     different kinds
Oyster sauce
Peanut oil
Rice
Sambal oelek
Sesame oil
Soy sauce: dark, light and
     sweetened
Tamarind pulp (dried) or purée in
     jars
Turmeric, ground

Spicy Chicken Soup
Soto Ayam

Serves 6

1 × 1.5 kg (3 lb) roasting chicken
2 litres (4 pints/8 cups) cold water
½ teaspoon whole black peppercorns
5 sprigs celery leaves
2 large brown onions
3 teaspoons salt
2 tablespoons peanut oil
2 salam leaves or 10 curry leaves
3 cloves garlic, chopped
1 teaspoon finely grated ginger
1 teaspoon dried shrimp paste
1 teaspoon ground turmeric
1 tablespoon ground coriander
2 teaspoons ground cumin
1 teaspoon ground fennel
½ teaspoon ground black pepper
½ teaspoon ground nutmeg

Garnishes
250 g (8 oz) egg noodles soaked in hot water for 10 minutes
3 hard-boiled eggs, diced
8 spring onions, chopped
3 tablespoons crisp-fried shallots
potato crisps

Joint the chicken and put into a large saucepan with the cold water to cover. Add the peppercorns, celery leaves, 1 whole onion and salt. Bring to the boil, then turn the heat to very low, cover and simmer for 40 minutes or until the chicken is tender. Remove from the heat and leave the chicken to cool in the liquid. When lukewarm, strain the stock into a bowl. Cut the chicken into small pieces and set aside, discarding the skin and bones.

Chop the remaining onion. Heat the oil in a pan and fry the onion with the salam leaves until the onion is soft and golden brown. Add the garlic, ginger, shrimp paste and ground spices. Crush the shrimp paste with the back of the frying spoon and after 1–2 minutes add the stock and simmer for 10 minutes.

Bring the soup to the boil and drop in the noodles for 3 minutes. Add the chicken pieces and ladle into a tureen. Garnish with the eggs, spring onions and fried shallots. Serve the soup with a separate bowl of potato crisps, which may be crumbled onto each serving of soup. For those who like it hot, offer a small bowl of sambal oelek on the side.

Spicy Satays

These little skewers of barbecued meat may be made using various kinds of meat and different kinds of marinade, but the marinade is always spicy and the sauce is always peanutty—a winning combination. Soak the bamboo skewers in cold water for at least a couple of hours before threading the meat on so they don't burn.

Makes about 30 skewers

750 g (1½ lb) chicken fillets (thigh or breast) or rump steak or pork loin
6–8 brown shallots or 2 brown onions, chopped
2 stems lemongrass, white portion only, thinly sliced
2 cloves garlic, chopped
2 teaspoons grated ginger or galangal
1 tablespoon ground coriander
2 teaspoons ground cumin
1 teaspoon ground turmeric
1 teaspoon salt
1 teaspoon brown sugar
2 tablespoons light soy sauce
2 tablespoons roasted, skinned peanuts
juice of ½ lime
1–2 tablespoons oil

To serve
Peanut Sauce (see page 45)
purple onions, sliced
lime wedges
cucumber, cut into batons

42

Cut the meat into small cubes, no larger than a fingertip. This gives a good proportion of spice marinade to meat, and ensures that the meat cooks through. The meat in satays is always well cooked.

Put the chopped shallots, lemongrass, garlic and ginger in a blender and process to a purée.

Roast the coriander and cumin in a dry pan over low heat, stirring constantly or shaking the pan to prevent scorching. This intensifies the flavour. Add to the blender with the turmeric, salt, sugar, soy sauce, peanuts and lime juice. Add 1 tablespoon oil and blend at high speed until a smooth purée results. Add the second spoonful of oil if necessary.

Pour the marinade over the meat, mix well, cover and leave for 1–2 hours. Thread the meat on soaked bamboo skewers, about 6 pieces on each, leaving a little space between so they cook evenly on all sides. Leave half the skewer bare and wrap in a strip of foil as extra protection against the skewer charring. Cook satays over glowing coals on a barbecue until the meat is well done. Serve with Peanut Sauce and purple onions, lime wedges and cucumber.

43

Vegetables with Peanut Sauce
Gado Gado

This popular salad of lightly cooked and raw vegetables served with Peanut Sauce is ideal for vegetarians if the shrimp paste is omitted. Adjust the quantities of vegetables as needed.

Serves 6–8

500 g new or waxy potatoes, boiled
500 g (1 lb) green beans or 2 bunches snake beans
3 carrots, sliced
250 g (8 oz) fresh beansprouts, tails pinched off
½ small cabbage, sliced and steamed
seedless cucumbers, sliced
firm bean curd, fried and sliced
hard-boiled eggs, quartered
Peanut Sauce (page 45)
crisp-fried shallots
prawn crackers (optional)

Peel and slice the potatoes into rounds. Trim the beans and cut into bite-sized pieces, then steam or blanch until tender but still crisp. Do the same with the carrots. Blanch the beansprouts in boiling water for a few seconds. Arrange all the vegetables on a platter, and top with slices of fried bean curd and the hard-boiled eggs.

Thin the Peanut Sauce with water to a thick pouring consistency. Taste and adjust the seasoning if necessary, then spoon over the vegetables. Sprinkle with fried shallots and garnish, if liked, with fried prawn crackers. Serve at room temperature.

NOTE: Seedless cucumbers are also known as Lebanese or telegraph cucumbers.

Peanut Sauce

There are many recipes for peanut sauce, but this is my favourite. If you have some crisp-fried shallots, sprinkle a couple of tablespoons on the sauce just before serving.

Makes about 500 ml (16 fl oz/2 cups)

125 ml (4 fl oz/½ cup) peanut oil
6 cloves garlic, sliced, or 2 teaspoons dried garlic flakes
1 medium-sized onion, sliced thinly or 2 tablespoons dried onion slices
3 large dried red chillies
1 teaspoon dried shrimp paste (*blacan*)
1 tablespoon tamarind purée or lemon juice
1 tablespoon soy sauce
375 g (12 oz) extra crunchy peanut butter
salt
1 tablespoon raw sugar

Heat the oil in a small wok over gentle heat. It should not be too hot. If using dried garlic flakes, put them in a fine wire strainer and lower into the oil for a few seconds just until they turn pale golden. Lift out and drain on absorbent paper. This is the only way to fry dried garlic without burning it. Do the same with the dried onion slices as they will also burn if left too long in the oil.

If using fresh onion and garlic, fry, stirring, until golden, then lift out on a slotted spoon and drain on absorbent paper until cool and crisp.

Fry the dried chillies until they puff and turn almost black. Drain and cool, then discard the stems and crumble the chillies into small pieces.

In the same oil, fry the shrimp paste, crushing it with the frying spoon. Add the tamarind and the soy sauce and stir to dissolve the shrimp paste. Remove from the heat and stir in the peanut butter until well combined. When the sauce is cold, mix in the garlic, onion, chilli and sugar. This mixture is too thick to pour. When required, stir in enough water or coconut milk to give a spooning or pouring consistency. Taste and add salt or extra sugar if necessary.

This sauce may be stored in the refrigerator for up to 2 weeks and used as required.

When time is short, stir 2 tablespoons of Charmaine Solomon's Rendang Curry Paste into 6 tablespoons of crunchy peanut butter and thin to a pouring consistency with cold water and/or canned coconut milk. My Rendang Curry Paste has more spices in it than this recipe for Peanut Sauce, but it tastes remarkably good. For texture, stir in 2 tablespoons of crisply fried shallots. In Asian stores, you can buy these already fried.

Fish Cakes in Banana Leaves
Otak Otak

A delicious appetiser of spiced fish enclosed in banana leaves and cooked over coals, often sold at street stalls in Indonesia and Malaysia. They are easily made with the help of a food processor. Aluminium foil can replace the banana leaves. If not using a barbecue, cook them under a preheated grill.

Makes 12 parcels

400 g (14 oz) boneless white fish fillets
3 tablespoons spice paste as in Laksa Lemak (see page 48) or
      Reuben Solomon's Singapore Laksa Paste
3 tablespoons coconut milk
1 egg, beaten
1 red chilli, seeded and sliced
finely grated zest of 1 lime
banana leaves

Slice the fish fillets and put into a food processor fitted with a steel blade. Mix together the laksa paste, coconut milk and egg. Process until the fish is finely chopped, adding the other ingredients through the feed tube until a well-combined mass forms. With a spatula, transfer the fish paste to a bowl and mix in the chilli and lime zest.

Wash the banana leaf and use a sharp knife to remove the thick centre rib. Cut the leaf into rectangles large enough to enclose a generous tablespoon of fish paste. To prevent the banana leaf splitting when folded, pass it over a gas flame or put it under an electric grill until it becomes pliable.

With a wet tablespoon, put heaped tablespoons of fish paste in the centre of each piece of banana leaf. Fold the leaf over to completely enclose the paste and flatten to less than 1 cm (½ in) thick. Fasten the ends with toothpicks. If banana leaves are not available, use a double layer of aluminium foil, shiny side in. When the parcels are all made, cook over a barbecue or under a griller until the fish paste is firm and cooked through, about 6 minutes on each side. Serve in the wrapping, which is removed before eating.

Curry Laksa
Laksa Lemak

A bowl of noodles swimming in a rich, spicy, coconut milk soup featuring whole prawns, slices of fried bean curd, snapping fresh beansprouts . . . this would have to be Singapore's signature dish. Other kinds of seafood may be used, or it may be made with chicken or fish. Laksa is a meal in one dish.

A photograph of this dish appears on page 51.

Serves 4–6

500 g (1 lb) raw king prawns
4 tablespoons peanut oil
2 litres (4 pints/8 cups) water
2 teaspoons salt
200 g (7 oz) rice vermicelli
400 ml (13 fl oz) coconut milk
small bunch laksa leaves (*polygonum*), shredded
8 squares deep-fried bean curd, sliced
1 small seedless cucumber, cut into narrow strips
150 g (5 oz) fresh beansprouts, trimmed and rinsed
3 hard-boiled eggs, halved

Spice Paste
10 purple shallots or 2 medium-sized onions, chopped
5 cloves garlic, peeled and crushed
5 candle (*kemiri*) nuts, roughly chopped
2 stems fresh lemongrass, finely sliced
3 tablespoons dried shrimp, soaked until softened
1 teaspoon dried shrimp paste (*blacan*)
2 tablespoons chopped galangal, fresh or in brine
2 teaspoons ground coriander
1 teaspoon ground turmeric
1 teaspoon chilli powder

48

Shell the prawns, leaving the tail on. Heat 1 tablespoon oil and stir-fry the shells and heads of the prawns until they turn red. Add the water and salt and bring to the boil. Cover and simmer for 20 minutes. Strain the stock and discard the heads and shells.

To make the Spice Paste, put all the ingredients into a blender and process until puréed, adding a little oil if necessary to facilitate blending.

Heat the remaining oil in a wok and fry the blended mixture over a low heat until fragrant, stirring constantly to make sure it does not scorch. When the oil separates from the mass and shines on the surface of the paste, add the strained stock. Bring to the boil and simmer for 20 minutes.

In another pan, cook the rice vermicelli for 2 minutes or until tender but do not overcook. Drain in a colander, run cool water through to stop them becoming too soft, and drain again.

Just before serving bring the soup to the simmering point and stir in the coconut milk. Add the prawns and cook only until they become opaque. Lift out on a slotted spoon and set aside. Drop the rice noodles into the soup to heat through, then ladle into large bowls.

Garnish each bowl with some of the shredded laksa leaves, fried bean curd and cucumber. Arrange the prawns on top, then a small handful of beansprouts and a halved hard-boiled egg. For those who like their laksa really hot, offer a small bowl of sambal oelek or crushed fresh chillies.

NOTE: Dried galangal slices are not suitable for using in the spice paste—they could do irreparable damage to your blender. Fresh or brined galangal are readily available in Asian shops.

For those who do not have time to prepare the spice paste from scratch, you can use Reuben Solomon's Singapore Laksa Paste. Dissolve half a jar (about 130 g/4 oz) in 1.25 litres (2½ pints/5 cups) hot water or stock. Cook 100 g (3½ oz) rice vermicelli in the soup and add prawns or thinly sliced chicken fillets, beansprouts, coconut milk and your favourite accompaniments. The quantities serve 3, and the rest of the paste will keep in the refrigerator for weeks.

49

Fried Noodles
Mee Goreng

There are many recipes for fried noodles, varying from region to region.
I chose one that illustrates the mixture of cultures found in south-east Asia.
I am indebted to my friend Wendy Hutton for this recipe from her book,
Singapore Food. She writes, 'A most unusual dish, sold by Indian hawkers . . .
a combination of Chinese, Indian and Western ingredients; makes a tasty
luncheon or snack.'

Serves 4–5

500 g (1 lb) fresh yellow noodles (*Hokkien mee*)
125 ml (4 fl oz/½ cup) oil
1 square hard bean curd, finely diced
1 medium-sized brown onion, chopped
1 medium-sized tomato, finely chopped
2 tablespoons coarsely chopped garlic chives or spring onions
1 sprig fresh curry leaves, finely chopped
2 tablespoons tomato sauce
1 tablespoon chilli sauce
2 teaspoons light soy sauce
2 eggs, lightly beaten
1 potato, boiled, peeled and finely diced
1 fresh green chilli, sliced

Rinse the noodles in warm water, drain and set aside.

Heat the oil in a wok and fry the bean curd until golden brown. Drain and
set aside.

Cook the onion in the same oil for 2–3 minutes until soft, then add the
drained noodles, tomato, chives, curry leaves and three sauces. Cook over a
gentle heat, stirring frequently, for 3–4 minutes.

Pour the beaten eggs over and leave to set for about 45 seconds before
stirring to mix it in well with the noodles. Add the potato and bean curd, stir,
cook for another 30 seconds and transfer to a large serving dish. Garnish with
green chilli and serve with additional tomato and chilli sauce on the side for
diners to add to taste.

Opposite page: Curry Laksa (see page 48)

Rice Noodles in Spicy Gravy
Mee Siam

Mee Siam is a dish reminiscent of the famous laksa (see page 48), but the noodles and gravy are served separately.

Serves 4–6

250 g (8 oz) rice vermicelli
200 g (7 oz) hard bean curd
oil for frying
250 g (8 oz) fresh beansprouts
250 g (8 oz) small cooked prawns, peeled and deveined
1 small bundle garlic chives or 6 spring onions, cut into bite-sized lengths
2 or 3 hard-boiled eggs, quartered
2 limes, quartered, or 6 *limau kesturi*, halved

Spice Paste
6 large dried red chillies
2 tablespoons small dried shrimp
6 brown shallots or 2 brown onions
3 cloves garlic
1 stem lemongrass, white portion only, thinly sliced
1 teaspoon dried shrimp paste (*blacan*)
2 tablespoons oil
1 tablespoon canned salted soybeans
1 teaspoon sugar
1 teaspoon salt
1 × 400 ml (13 fl oz) can coconut milk
walnut-sized piece of dried tamarind or 2 tablespoons tamarind purée

Drop the rice vermicelli into a large pan of boiling water, boil for 2 minutes, drain in a colander and run cold water through to stop cooking. Drain again.

Cut the bean curd into 1 cm (½ in) thick slices, press on paper towels to absorb the excess moisture and fry in oil until golden on both sides. Drain, cool and dice.

Wash the beansprouts and pinch off any straggly tails. Set aside.

To make the Spice Paste, soak the dried chillies and dried shrimp in enough hot water to cover for 15 minutes. Put in an electric blender with 2 tablespoons of the soaking water and the shallots, garlic, lemongrass and shrimp paste. Blend to a purée, adding a little of the oil if necessary.

Heat the 2 tablespoons oil in a wok and on low heat fry the purée, stirring constantly for about 3 minutes, until fragrant. Add the soybeans, sugar and salt.

Remove half the cooked paste to a saucepan, stir in the coconut milk and the same amount of water. Soak the dried tamarind in about 125 ml (4 fl oz/ ½ cup) hot water and, when softened, knead to dissolve the pulp. Strain the liquid and add to the saucepan, stirring constantly while bringing to simmering point. If using tamarind purée, just add and simmer, uncovered, for a few minutes.

Reheat the remaining paste and toss the prawns, beansprouts and chives for 1 minute. Add the drained rice vermicelli, toss and stir until well combined and heated through. Transfer to a serving dish and garnish with the fried bean curd, eggs and limes.

Serve the hot gravy in a separate deep dish so each person can take a serving of rice noodles, then ladle the gravy over. For extra flavour, squeeze a little lime juice into the gravy. A small dish of sliced fresh chillies or a hot sambal may be served alongside.

NOTE: *Limau kesturi* are also known as Chinese limes, *citrus microcarpa* and *kalamansi*.

On a recent visit to Singapore, I enjoyed this dish and craved it when I was back home, but could not spare the time to prepare it. However, where there's a will there's a way. I put the eggs on to boil, and created a very good reproduction of this dish in minutes. In 1.5 litres (3 pints/6 good cups) boiling water, I dissolved 3 tablespoons Reuben Solomon's Singapore Laksa Paste and 2 tablespoons Charmaine Solomon's Rendang Curry Paste plus 1 tablespoon sugar to give the sweetness which was so appealing in the Singapore version. Our garden yielded chives and limes, the pantry always has rice vermicelli and cans of coconut milk. I didn't even miss the tofu and bean sprouts, but I did wish I hadn't used up all the prawns in the freezer. For a 10-minute meal, it was great!

53

Fried Fresh Rice Noodles
Char Kway Teow

A popular dish that definitely tells of the Chinese influence in South-east Asia. Fresh rice noodles are sold at Chinese shops as *sa hor fun* and Vietnamese shops as *banh pho*. Sometimes, they are sold already cut into strips.

Serves 6

1 kg (2 lb) fresh rice noodles (*kway teow*)
6 dried shiitake mushrooms
250 g (8 oz) pork with plenty of fat
2 Chinese sausages (*lap cheong*)
3 cloves garlic, chopped
3 hot red chillies, sliced
4 shallots or 1 small onion, sliced
100 g (3½ oz) barbecued pork fillet, sliced
250 g (8 oz) raw prawns, shelled and deveined
200 g (7 oz) cleaned squid, cut into strips (optional)
125 g (4 oz) fresh beansprouts, tails removed
2 tablespoons light soy sauce
1 tablespoon dark soy sauce
1 tablespoon oyster sauce
2 eggs, beaten
3 spring onions, chopped

If using uncut rice noodles, cut into strips about a finger's width. Place in a colander and pour boiling water over them. Leave to drain.

Soak the mushrooms in very hot water for 20 minutes. Squeeze out the water, discard the stems and cut the caps into strips. Cut the pork into 2 cm (¾ in) pieces and fry in a wok without any oil until the fat runs. Lift out the pork pieces and leave 2 tablespoons of the melted fat in the wok, reserving the rest. Steam the Chinese sausages for 10 minutes, then cut into very thin diagonal slices.

Reheat the pork fat in the wok and on low heat fry the garlic, chillies and shallots until golden and fragrant. Add the pork, mushrooms, Chinese sausages, barbecued pork, prawns and squid and toss on high heat for 2 minutes. Add the beansprouts and toss for 30 seconds, then remove the mixture from the wok.

Heat another 2 tablespoons melted pork fat until smoking hot. Add the drained rice noodles and toss until heated through. Pour over all the sauces and stir-fry until well mixed. Push noodles to the side of the wok, pour the beaten eggs into the centre and stir until set. Return the fried mixture to the wok together with the spring onions and toss again until heated through.

Fried Rice
Nasi Goreng

Another recipe for fried rice (see also page 133), a dish as flexible as you want it to be, mostly depending on what you find in the refrigerator, so long as one of the finds is cold cooked rice. From there on, the possibilities are endless. Chicken or barbecued pork may take the place of prawns and beef, even leftover curry can be used—a fairly dry curry is better than one with lots of gravy. For an Indonesian version of nasi goreng, a fried egg, sunny side up, must top each portion.

Serves 2–4

4 cups cold cooked rice
2 eggs, beaten
salt and pepper
3 tablespoons oil
3 shallots or 1 onion, finely sliced
1 teaspoon finely chopped garlic
1 teaspoon dried shrimp paste (*blacan*)
250 g (8 oz) rump steak, thinly sliced
250 g (8 oz) small raw or cooked school prawns, peeled and deveined
1 tablespoon sweet soy sauce
6 spring onions, thinly sliced
2 fresh chillies, seeded and sliced
1 fried egg per person (optional)
1 seedless cucumber, finely sliced

Separate the rice grains with wet hands so they don't clump together. Season the beaten eggs with salt and pepper to taste, and cook 2 flat omelettes in a lightly oiled pan. Cut the omelettes into thin shreds and set aside.

Heat the oil in a wok and fry the shallots and garlic until fragrant and golden. Add the shrimp paste and fry for a further minute, then stir-fry the steak until it changes colour. Add the prawns and stir-fry until opaque. Add the rice and toss, sprinkling with the soy sauce. Add spring onions and chillies, and continue tossing over heat until the ingredients are well mixed and heated through. Toss the omelette strips through the rice. Serve with a fried egg on each portion if desired, and slices of cucumber to garnish.

55

Coconut Rice
Nasi Lemak

This recipe does not work in a rice cooker.

Serves 6–8

500 g (1 lb) medium or short-grain rice
400 ml (13 fl oz) canned coconut milk
300 ml (10 fl oz) water
2 teaspoons salt
a strip of fresh pandan leaf (optional)

Wash and drain the rice well. In a saucepan with a heavy base and well-fitting lid bring the coconut milk, water, salt and pandan leaf to the boil on low heat, stirring. Add the rice, turn the heat to very low, cover tightly and cook for 20 minutes. If necessary, put a heat diffuser under the pan so the rice does not scorch. When all the coconut milk is absorbed turn off the heat and leave the pot covered for 10 minutes. Turn the rice into a steamer or colander and steam over boiling water for a further 20 minutes, gradually turning the heat down so that the water only simmers. Serve as an accompaniment to dishes such as Beef Rendang (see page 64), Hot Prawn Sambal (see page 60), Thai Fish Cakes (see page 6), Greens with Shrimp Paste (see page 65), and Balinese-style Fried Chicken (see page 63).

Spicy Yellow Rice
Nasi Kuning

Bright yellow with turmeric and subtly flavoured with whole spices, this rich rice cooked in coconut milk is usually served when entertaining.

This recipe does not work in a rice cooker.

Serves 10–12

1 kg (2 lb) long-grain rice
1 tablespoon ghee
2 tablespoons oil
2 medium-sized onions, thinly sliced
2 cloves garlic, chopped
1 small cinnamon quill
5 cardamom pods, bruised
5 whole cloves
2 level teaspoons ground turmeric
2 litres (4 pints/8 cups) thin coconut milk (see Note)
3 teaspoons salt

Wash the rice and leave to drain for 1 hour. In a heavy saucepan heat the ghee and oil and fry the onions and garlic until golden brown. Add the whole spices and fry for 1–2 minutes. Add the turmeric and stir for a few seconds, then add the rice and stir over medium heat for 3 minutes or until all the grains are coated with oil. Add the coconut milk and salt. Bring to the boil, lower the heat, cover the pan tightly and steam the rice for 15–20 minutes.

After the first 10 minutes put a heat diffuser under the pan so the bottom does not scorch. Turn off the heat and leave the rice covered for a further 10 minutes.

For special occasions, serve the rice garnished with sultanas and cashews or slivered almonds that have been fried until golden.

NOTE: Thin coconut milk refers to the second extract if you are making coconut milk from scratch, but may be approximated by diluting canned coconut milk with an equal amount of water or even more than an equal amount if the canned milk is very thick. It is preferable to use diluted coconut milk since it is very high in saturated fat.

Chilli Crab

Malaysia and Singapore vie with each other for the best crab dishes, and often import live crabs from Sri Lanka, a fact they proudly advertise outside the restaurants. A chef dispatches the live crustaceans only when customers order the signature dish and are sitting waiting to be served. Chilli crab and black pepper crab are two famous dishes, with chilli crab perhaps the better known. This feast requires hands-on participation to reach the sweet flesh.

Serves 4

2 mud crabs or 4 blue swimmer crabs
125 ml (4 fl oz/½ cup) peanut oil
1 tablespoon finely chopped ginger
3 teaspoons finely chopped garlic
3 fresh red chillies, seeded and chopped
125 ml (4 fl oz/½ cup) tomato sauce (ketchup)
125 ml (4 fl oz/½ cup) chilli sauce
1 tablespoon light soy sauce
60 ml (2 fl oz/¼ cup) water
1 tablespoon sugar
1 teaspoon salt or to taste
2 teaspoons salted black beans (optional)
1 egg, beaten
4 spring onions, finely chopped

Wash the crabs, scrubbing away any mossy patches on the shell. Put the point of a knife under the 'apron', which is on the underside of the crab, twist slightly and pull away the dark stomach portion. Discard. Remove the carapace (hard top shell) as well as the gills, the feathery grey tissue known as 'dead men's fingers'. Use a heavy chopper to cut the crab into halves or quarters. Crack the claws so the flesh is easier to get at.

Heat the oil in a wok until very hot. Fry the crab pieces, a few at a time, until they change colour, turning them in the oil. Remove each lot as they turn red. When all the crab pieces are fried, turn the heat to low and fry the ginger, garlic and chillies, stirring, until soft and golden. Add the sauces, water, sugar, salt and black beans. Return the crab pieces to the wok and let them simmer in the sauce for 5 minutes, with the lid on. Uncover and dribble in the beaten egg, toss in the spring onions, and cook without stirring until the egg sets. Serve with steamed rice.

A quick way to cook this dish is to buy cooked crabs and clean them as described. Then heat a jar of Reuben Solomon's Singapore Chilli Crab Paste with an equal amount of water. Add the crab pieces and simmer for 3 minutes or until heated through. Lift the crabs onto a serving platter. Add the spring onions and slowly pour the beaten egg into the sauce. When it sets, spoon over the crab and serve.

Hot Prawn Sambal
Sambal Udang Asam

Serves 6

500 g (1 lb) raw prawns
2 teaspoons dried tamarind pulp or 3 tablespoons tamarind purée
4 brown shallots or 1 onion, finely chopped
3 teaspoons finely chopped garlic
1 teaspoon finely chopped ginger
2 teaspoons finely chopped fresh galangal or 2 slices galangal in brine
6 fresh red chillies or 2 tablespoons sambal oelek
1 stem lemongrass, white portion only, thinly sliced
2 tablespoons peanut oil
2 teaspoons palm sugar or brown sugar
½ teaspoon salt or to taste

Shell and devein the prawns. If they are large, cut each into 3–4 pieces.

If using dried tamarind, soak in 125 ml (4 fl oz/½ cup) hot water for 10 minutes, then squeeze to dissolve the pulp. Strain and reserve the liquid, discarding the seeds and fibres.

Pound or blend the shallots, garlic, ginger, galangal, chillies and lemongrass until a paste forms.

Heat the oil in a wok and fry the blended mixture, stirring, until cooked and fragrant.

Toss in the prawns and stir-fry until opaque. Add the tamarind liquid and simmer until thick. Stir in the sugar and salt and serve as a piquant accompaniment to rice and curries.

Stir-fried Prawns in Shells

There is a well-patronised restaurant in Singapore that offers only three specialties. This is one of them. All the ingredients may be prepared ahead of time, leaving only the quick cooking to be done just before serving.

Serves 4–6

750 g (1½ lb) large tiger prawns
4 tablespoons peanut oil
4 spring onions, cut into bite-sized lengths
3 red chillies, seeded and sliced
4 slices ginger, finely shredded
3 large cloves garlic, finely chopped

Sauce
2 tablespoons Chinese wine
3 tablespoons light soy sauce
1 tablespoon sugar
2 teaspoons dark sesame oil

The prawns should have the sandy tract removed, and it is possible to do this while leaving the shells on. Make a small incision in the prawn above the tail segment. From just below the head, grasp the other end of the sandy tract and carefully draw out the whole length. Rinse the prawns briefly in cold water, then dry them well on kitchen paper.

To make the Sauce, combine all the ingredients in a small bowl, stirring to dissolve the sugar.

Heat a wok, add the oil and when very hot add the prawns and stir-fry on high heat until they turn red. Push the prawns to the side of the wok, toss in the spring onions, chillies, ginger and garlic and continue to stir-fry for less than a minute. Add the sauce ingredients and toss everything together for a further minute, then serve at once.

Chicken in Coconut Milk

Serves 6

1.5 kg (3 lb) chicken thigh cutlets and drumsticks
2 teaspoons crushed garlic
2 teaspoons finely grated ginger
1 tablespoon pounded galangal, fresh or in brine
1 tablespoon finely grated candle (*kemiri*) nuts or macadamias
1 tablespoon ground coriander
2 teaspoons ground cumin
1 teaspoon ground fennel
1 teaspoon salt
½ teaspoon ground black pepper
4 tablespoons oil
3 brown onions, finely sliced
1 x 400 ml (13 fl oz) can coconut milk
1 stem lemongrass, whole, bruised
1 small cinnamon quill
juice of ½ lime or 2 teaspoons tamarind purée

Put the chicken pieces into a bowl.

Make a mixture of the garlic, ginger, galangal, nuts, coriander, cumin, fennel, salt and pepper. Mix in just enough oil to give the spices a spreadable consistency and rub over the chicken. Cover and set aside for 1 hour.

Heat the oil in a wok or frying pan and fry the onions slowly until they become golden brown. This will take some time, and they should be stirred frequently so they cook evenly. Lift out on a slotted spoon and set aside. Add a little extra oil to the pan if necessary and fry the chicken pieces on medium heat until they are golden on all sides.

Shake the can of coconut milk well before opening. Dilute half the coconut milk with 300 ml (10 fl oz) water and pour over the chicken. Add the lemongrass and cinnamon. Stir until the mixture comes to a boil, then reduce the heat and cook uncovered for 30 minutes or until the chicken is tender. Add the remaining coconut milk, stir well and cook for a further 10 minutes. Do not cover the chicken at any stage. Stir in the lime juice or tamarind. Taste and see if extra salt is needed. Before serving, remove the cinnamon stick and lemongrass. Garnish with the reserved fried onions. Serve with white rice, vegetables and sambals.

Balinese-style Fried Chicken

Serves 6

2 small spatchcock
peanut oil for frying
2 brown onions, roughly chopped
6 cloves garlic
1 tablespoon chopped ginger
4–6 hot red chillies, sliced
6 candle (*kemiri*) nuts or macadamias, finely chopped
2 tablespoons sweet soy sauce (*ketjap manis*)
2 teaspoons palm sugar or brown sugar
2 tablespoons lime juice
1 teaspoon salt
300 ml (10 fl oz) coconut milk

Cut the spatchcock into quarters and dry well on paper towels.

Heat the peanut oil in a wok or heavy frying pan and fry a few pieces of chicken at a time until nicely browned. Remove from the pan as they are done, and drain on absorbent paper.

In a blender purée the onions, garlic, ginger, chillies, nuts and soy sauce. If necessary add a little oil to facilitate blending.

Pour off the oil from the wok or frying pan, leaving only 1–2 tablespoons. Fry the blended mixture, stirring constantly, until it is fragrant. Add sugar, lime juice, salt and coconut milk, stirring until the mixture comes to the boil. Return the chicken pieces and simmer uncovered until the chicken is tender and gravy reduced. Serve with Coconut Rice (see page 56) or Spicy Yellow Rice (see page 57) and other accompaniments.

Beef Rendang

I have used this recipe so often that the page in my kitchen copy of the *Complete Asian Cookbook* is bespattered and stained. Now, however, I simply use my Rendang Curry Paste since it contains all the ingredients that contribute to the spicy flavour. This dish needs long simmering. It keeps well, so it is a good idea to make more than you need for a meal and refrigerate the rest for a week or freeze for longer periods.

Serves 10–12

2 kg (4 lb) stewing steak
1 teaspoon ground aromatic ginger (*kencur*)
125 ml (4 fl oz/½ cup) tamarind liquid
3 teaspoons palm sugar or brown sugar

Paste
2 brown onions, chopped
6 cloves garlic, peeled
1 tablespoon finely grated ginger
6–8 fresh red chillies, seeded and sliced
2 stems fresh lemongrass, white portion only, finely sliced
1 tablespoon chopped galangal, fresh or in brine
125 ml (4 fl oz/½ cup) water
1 × 560 ml (19 fl oz) can coconut milk
2 teaspoons salt
2 teaspoons ground turmeric
3 teaspoons chilli powder or to taste
4 teaspoons ground coriander
1 teaspoon ground cumin
1 teaspoon ground fennel

Cut the beef into strips about 3 cm (1¼ in) wide and 6 cm (2½ in) long and put into a large saucepan.

To make the Paste, blend the onions, garlic, ginger, chillies, lemongrass, galangal and water until smooth. Pour into a saucepan together with the coconut milk, salt, ground spices and ground aromatic ginger.

Stir while bringing to the boil, then reduce the heat, add the tamarind liquid and simmer, uncovered, for 2 hours or more. When the beef is tender and the oil separates from the gravy, add the sugar and stir constantly, letting the meat fry in the oily gravy until it is a dark brown.

Serve with rice, vegetables and sambals.

You can use Charmaine Solomon's Rendang Curry Paste to save making the Paste yourself—just add 1 can (560 ml/19 fl oz) coconut milk to the paste. Use 6 tablespoons paste to 2 kg (4 lb) meat.

Greens with Shrimp Paste

The favourite green vegetable throughout Asia is probably water convolvulus, probably better known in Malay as *kangkung* or in Chinese as *oong choy*. It can be steamed like spinach or simmered in coconut milk, but more likely it will be combined with the flavours of the region, including the ubiquitous shrimp paste.

Serves 4

1 kg (2 lb) water spinach or other leafy greens
1 teaspoon dried shrimp paste (*blacan*)
2 tablespoons small dried shrimp
1 brown onion, chopped
3 cloves garlic
2 teaspoons finely grated ginger
2 red chillies, finely chopped
3 tablespoons peanut oil
salt
2 teaspoons sugar

Wash the greens thoroughly. Discard the bottom end of the stems, which could be tough. Cut the rest into short lengths, about 5 cm (2 in).

Wrap the shrimp paste in foil and grill for about 2 minutes on each side.

Put the dried shrimp in a blender and blend on high speed until they are reduced to a floss. Add the onion, garlic, ginger, chillies and a little oil or water to make blending easier, and blend until combined.

Heat the oil in a wok and fry the paste, stirring, until it smells fragrant. Then add the shrimp paste and crush with spoon, then add 125 ml (4 fl oz/ ½ cup) water and dissolve. Toss in the green vegetable, cover and steam for 3 minutes or until it is tender. Season to taste with salt and sugar, mixing well. Serve with rice and curries.

Vegetables in Coconut Milk
Sayur Lodeh

A useful recipe for any vegetable in season. Pumpkin, beans, broccoli, cabbage, zucchini and snow peas may be used singly or in combination, adding them according to the time required for them to become tender.

Serves 6

500 g (1 lb) vegetables
2 tablespoons peanut oil
1 onion, finely chopped
2 teaspoons chopped garlic
1 fresh red or green chilli, seeded
1 teaspoon dried shrimp paste
1 stem lemongrass, whole, bruised
500 ml (16 fl oz/2 cups) vegetable or chicken stock
250 ml (8 fl oz/1 cup) coconut milk
salt
1 tablespoon lime or lemon juice

Cut the large vegetables into bite-sized pieces.
    Heat the oil in a saucepan and fry the onion until soft and golden. Add the garlic, chilli and shrimp paste and fry on low heat, crushing the shrimp paste with the spoon. Add the lemongrass, stock and coconut milk. Simmer uncovered for a few minutes, then add vegetables and cook until tender. Add salt to taste. Stir in the lime juice and serve hot with rice and other dishes.

Moulded Sago Pudding
Gula Melaka

People either love sago or hate it, but even the most reluctant person with memories of 'nursery food' will agree that when served like this, with coconut milk and palm honey, it is a dessert that finishes off a hot, spicy meal to perfection.

Serves 6–8

2.5 litres (5 pints/10 cups) water
300 g (10 oz) sago
2 tablespoons fresh milk
250 ml (8 fl oz) palm honey or 250 g (8 oz) palm sugar (*gula melaka*)
300 ml (10 fl oz) coconut milk
¼ teaspoon salt

Bring the water to a rolling boil and slowly add the sago. Boil uncovered for 7–10 minutes, then turn off the heat, cover the pan tightly and let it sit for 10 minutes. The grains of sago should be clear at the end of this time, otherwise leave for a while longer. Run cold water into the pan, stir well and pour the sago into a sieve, shaking the sieve so the water runs out. Pour the sago into a bowl and stir in the milk. This takes away the grey colour that makes sago unappetising. Pour into a serving dish or individual dishes and refrigerate.

If you cannot find palm honey, chop the palm sugar into small pieces and heat gently with 125 ml (4 fl oz/½ cup) water. When dissolved, strain through a fine sieve (a tea strainer is ideal) to remove any impurities.

Stir the salt into the coconut milk to bring out the flavour.

Serve the sago pudding with the palm honey or palm sugar syrup and coconut milk at room temperature—chilling will solidify the fat.

Black Rice Porridge
Pulut Hitam

A favourite sweet in Singapore, Malaysia and Indonesia, served warm like porridge, with a splash of coconut milk. The rice itself has a subtle fragrance, but add a slice of ginger or strip of fresh pandan leaf when simmering, if you like. Nonyas add dried longans when cooking the rice.

Serves 6–8

1 cup black glutinous rice
2 litres (4 pints/8 cups) water
60 g (2 oz) palm sugar, chopped
3 tablespoons brown sugar
5 slices ginger or 20 cm (8 in) strip pandan leaf or 20 dried longans
250 ml (8 fl oz/1 cup) thick coconut milk
¼ teaspoon salt

Wash the rice in several changes of cold water and drain well. Put into a saucepan with the water and bring to the boil. Cover and simmer for 30 minutes. Add both kinds of sugar and the ginger, pandan or longan—whatever you choose to flavour the porridge. Cook until the rice grains are very tender, about 40 minutes. Stir now and then to prevent rice sticking to the bottom of the pan, and add more boiling water if the porridge becomes too thick.

Serve warm, with a little lightly salted coconut milk poured over.

69

India and Sri Lanka

THE AROMAS AND spicy flavours of the Indian sub-continent and its neighbour, Sri Lanka, are very similar, though there are differences which give each their individuality.

In India alone, there are distinctions between the food of north and south, east and west. Generally, northern food is not as hot or pungent, but certainly richer because it is cooked in ghee. It is often the cooking medium that makes the flavour difference in the food of India's many regions. There is no mistaking whether a dish has been cooked in mustard seed oil, a favourite in eastern India; in coconut oil in South India and Sri Lanka; or in ghee, favoured in central and north India. Peanut oil is also used, mainly in Maharashtra and Gujarat. Since it is nearly odourless once refined, it can be used to cook the food of any region.

Don't get hung up on whether you have the 'right' kind of oil in your pantry. Any vegetable oil may be used, except perhaps strongly fruity virgin olive oil with its distinctive flavour, which would be at variance with the flavours of Asia. In dishes such as Butter Chicken (see page 97), it would be ridiculous not to use clarified butter (ghee) or butter. But instead of using all ghee or butter with its in-built saturated fat, I use a proportion of it for giving the right flavour, mixed with pure olive oil or light olive oil. Since I don't really care for the flavour of coconut oil, nor the fact that it is highly saturated (as is palm oil), I use canola, peanut, grapeseed or sunflower oil. I avoid blended oils because I don't know what is in them exactly. Even the most assiduous reader of labels doesn't always find the information sought.

A large proportion of the population of India and, to a lesser extent, Sri Lanka, is vegetarian. Their diet is based on grains, lentils and

71

vegetables. In India, milk products such as fresh home-made cheese and yoghurt contribute protein. In certain areas fish is eaten, being termed 'fruit of the sea'. Meat and poultry are enjoyed by those whose religion does not forbid the eating of flesh.

North Indians eat lamb, Sri Lankans eat beef and pork and sometimes mutton (goat), but lamb is not raised in the tropics. Lamb is very suitable for curries, as its richness is tempered by the spices. Most of the classic North Indian dishes such as korma and raan would not work with another meat.

There are many taboos, for both religious and aesthetic reasons.

Hindus will not eat beef, Muslims will not eat pork. Among the Christian and Parsi communities there are no such taboos.

Roti is a general term for Indian breads. Chapatis are disks of unleavened bread cooked on a dry griddle. Puris are the same disks deep-fried in hot oil until puffed and golden. Parathas are flat bread layered with ghee. A good substitute for parathas are wheat tortillas, available from the supermarket, heated briefly in a dry frying pan or with just a little ghee. Naan is a leavened bread. Making naan is a long process, so it's easiest to buy it from your local Indian take-away.

RECOMMENDED PANTRY

Basmati Rice
Black mustard seeds
Cardamom, whole pods and ground
Chillies (dried) and chilli powder
Cinnamon quills
Cloves, whole and ground
Coconut, desiccated
Coconut milk, canned
Coriander seeds, whole and ground
Cumin seeds, whole and ground
Curry leaves, dried
Fennel seeds, whole and ground
Fenugreek seeds, whole and ground

Garam Masala (see page 168)
Ghee
Lentils
Mace, ground
Maldive fish
Nigella seeds, whole
Nutmeg, whole
Panch Phora (see page 170)
Pandan leaves, dried, fresh or frozen
Peppercorns, black, whole
Saffron, whole strands and ground
Tamarind pulp, dried
Turmeric, ground

Pepper Water
Rasam

Sipped at the end of a meal or spooned over rice, this soup is a digestive, much prized by those who enjoy South Indian food.

Serves 4

1 tablespoon tamarind pulp or 3 tablespoons tamarind purée
250 ml (8 fl oz/1 cup) hot water
2 cloves garlic, sliced
½ teaspoon ground black pepper
1 teaspoon ground cumin
1 litre (2 pints/4 cups) cold water
2 teaspoons salt
2 tablespoons chopped fresh coriander
2 teaspoons oil
1 teaspoon black mustard seeds
a sprig of fresh curry leaves

Put the tamarind pulp in a bowl, pour over the hot water and leave for 10 minutes to soften. Squeeze to dissolve the pulp in the water, strain and discard the seeds and fibres. If using tamarind purée or instant tamarind, stir into 250 ml (8 fl oz/1 cup) hot water to dissolve.

In a non-aluminium saucepan put the tamarind liquid, garlic, pepper, cumin, cold water, salt and coriander. Bring to the boil, then turn the heat down and simmer for 10 minutes.

In a small saucepan heat the oil and fry mustard seeds and curry leaves until the seeds pop and the leaves are brown. Add to the simmering soup and serve.

Mulligatawny

Who has not heard of mulligatawny, that derivation of a simple South Indian digestive soup that has been adapted to become something far richer and more robust? Mulligatawny, as Europeans know it, is a hybrid dish. It is the Anglo-Indian version of a very simple soup known as 'pepper water'. (In the Tamil language, *molagu* means pepper and *thanni* means water.) The colonising British would not have enjoyed pepper water in its original form. The cooks in their employ (who were brilliant at adapting dishes to suit their masters' tastebuds) added meat or chicken, the richness of coconut milk and onions or shallots fried in ghee as a final finishing touch.

Going one step further, grand hotels in the sub-continent and neighbouring lands adopted the 'curry tiffin'—a long and leisurely lunch starting with mulligatawny. The soup can be based on chicken, beef or mutton, variations which would have horrified the vegetarian originators. As served to Europeans, often there was a mound of rice ladled into the middle of the soup plate that held the mulligatawny. Not content with that, some cooks offered side dishes of quartered hard-boiled eggs, fresh grated coconut, lime wedges and crumbled fried bacon. Truly a case of gilding the lily, and a far cry from what 'pepper water' started out to be, but there is no denying its popularity.

Serves 6–8

1 kg (2 lb) gravy beef or best end of lamb neck
1 kg (2 lb) soup bones
1 large onion, stuck with 4 cloves
3 cloves garlic, peeled and left whole
4 slices fresh ginger, finely chopped
2 teaspoons whole black peppercorns
6–8 cardamom pods, bruised
2 tablespoons coriander seeds or ground coriander
1 tablespoon cumin seeds or ground cumin
1 teaspoon ground turmeric
½ teaspoon chilli powder (optional)
2 teaspoons salt
1 tablespoon dried tamarind pulp

Tempering

1 tablespoon ghee

4 shallots or 2 small onions, finely sliced

½ teaspoon black mustard seeds

a sprig of fresh curry leaves (about 12)

1 × 400 ml (13 fl oz) can coconut milk

a squeeze of lime or lemon juice (optional)

Put the beef and soup bones into a large saucepan with sufficient cold water to cover. Add the onion, garlic, ginger, spices, salt and tamarind pulp. Bring to the boil, reduce the heat and simmer gently for about 2 hours, skimming from time to time. The meat should be tender and the liquid reduced. Cool slightly, remove the meat from the stock and finely dice. Set aside. Pour the stock through a fine strainer and discard the spices. There should be about 1.5 litres (3 pint/6 cups) stock.

Finishing the mulligatawny is a process known as 'tempering'. Heat the ghee and fry the shallots until a dark golden brown. Add the mustard seeds and curry leaves and fry for a minute or two longer. Pour the hot stock into the pan, taking care because it will sputter. Simmer for 5 minutes. Just before serving, stir in the coconut milk. Taste and adjust the seasoning with salt and, if liked, a good squeeze of lime or lemon juice.

Return the diced meat to the pan and heat through without boiling. Serve hot.

Spiced Rice and Lentils
Kitchri

'Kedgeree' is the perfect example of British–Indian food. It appears on breakfast tables, with flaked smoked fish and hard-boiled eggs added. The original dish is kitchri, one of the most popular home-style dishes in the Indian sub-continent—a well balanced, complete meal of delicately spiced rice and lentils. While some families prefer plain steamed rice served with a separate dish of lentils (Dhal, see page 77) kitchri needs only a little yoghurt and perhaps a spoonful of chutney to accompany it.

Serves 4–6

1½ cups long-grain rice, preferably basmati
1 cup red lentils
2 tablespoons ghee or oil
2 medium-sized onions, finely sliced
1 cinnamon quill
5 whole green cardamom pods, bruised
5 whole cloves
few whole black peppercorns
825 ml (27 fl oz/3½ cups) hot water
2 teaspoons salt

Wash the rice and drain well for at least 30 minutes. Wash the lentils well and drain thoroughly.

Heat the ghee in a saucepan and fry the onions on medium heat until golden brown. Remove and reserve two-thirds of the fried onion for garnishing the finished dish.

Add the rice, lentils and whole spices to the onions in the pan and fry, stirring, for 2–3 minutes. Add the hot water and salt, bring to the boil, then cover and cook on low heat for 15 minutes without lifting the lid. Turn off the heat and leave the pan covered for a further 10 minutes. Fluff the rice with a fork, remove the whole spices and serve the kitchri garnished with fried onion and accompanied by fruit chutney and a bowl of thick yoghurt or Cucumber Raita (see page 89).

Dhal

The ever-present lentil purée served with rice or chapatis may be made with many different kinds of lentils, but the common and easily available red lentil is perhaps the most popular because it is quick to cook. Other types of lentils should be soaked for a few hours before cooking.

Serves 6

250 g (8 oz) red lentils
2 tablespoons ghee or oil
2 large onions, finely sliced
2 cloves garlic, chopped
1 teaspoon finely grated fresh ginger
1 teaspoon ground turmeric
750 ml (24 fl oz/3 cups) hot water
1 teaspoon salt
½ teaspoon Garam Masala (see page 168)

Wash the lentils well in several changes of cold water, discarding any that float. Drain the lentils in a sieve.

In a heavy saucepan heat the ghee and fry the onions until golden brown. Remove half the onions and set aside for garnish. Add the garlic and ginger and fry a few seconds longer. Add the turmeric and stir, then add the lentils and stir for a couple of minutes. Add the hot water and bring to the boil. Turn the heat to low, cover and simmer for 20 minutes or until the lentils are half cooked. Add salt and garam masala, mix well and cook until the lentils are soft and puréed. If the mixture is too liquid, cook uncovered to evaporate some of the water. Serve garnished with the reserved fried onions.

Vegetable and Lentil Soup
Sambar

If you go to an Indian vegetarian restaurant, chances are you will be served a small bowl of this vegetable and lentil soup with whatever you order—steamed lentil dumplings, crisp lentil pancakes or simply with rice and vegetable curries. You don't ask for it—it appears, magically, on your banana leaf platter or metal tray.

Serves 6

1 cup split peas or red lentils
1.5 litres (3 pints/6 cups) water
1 tablespoon tamarind pulp or instant tamarind
250 ml (8 fl oz/1 cup) hot water
2 tablespoons oil
1 tablespoon ground coriander
2 teaspoons ground cumin
½ teaspoon ground black pepper
½ teaspoon ground turmeric
a pinch of chilli powder
¼ teaspoon asafoetida
3 cups mixed diced vegetables
2 fresh green chillies, seeded and sliced
2 teaspoons salt or to taste
½ teaspoon black mustard seeds
1 small onion, finely sliced

Wash the lentils and soak overnight or for at least 2 hours. Drain and cook with the measured water, simmering until soft.

Put the tamarind pulp in a bowl, pour over the hot water and leave for 10 minutes to soften. Squeeze to dissolve the pulp in the water, strain and discard the seeds and fibres. If using tamarind purée or instant tamarind, stir into 250 ml (8 fl oz/1 cup) hot water to dissolve. Add the tamarind liquid to the lentils.

In another pan large enough to hold all the lentils, heat 1 tablespoon oil and fry the ground spices and asafoetida on low heat, stirring, for 1–2 minutes. Pour the lentil mixture into this pan, add the vegetables and chillies and simmer until the vegetables are cooked. Season with salt.

Heat the remaining tablespoon of oil in a small saucepan and fry the mustard seeds and onions until the seeds pop and the onion is brown. Add to the soup, simmer a few minutes longer and serve. Sambar should be fairly thick, with a pronounced sour and hot flavour.

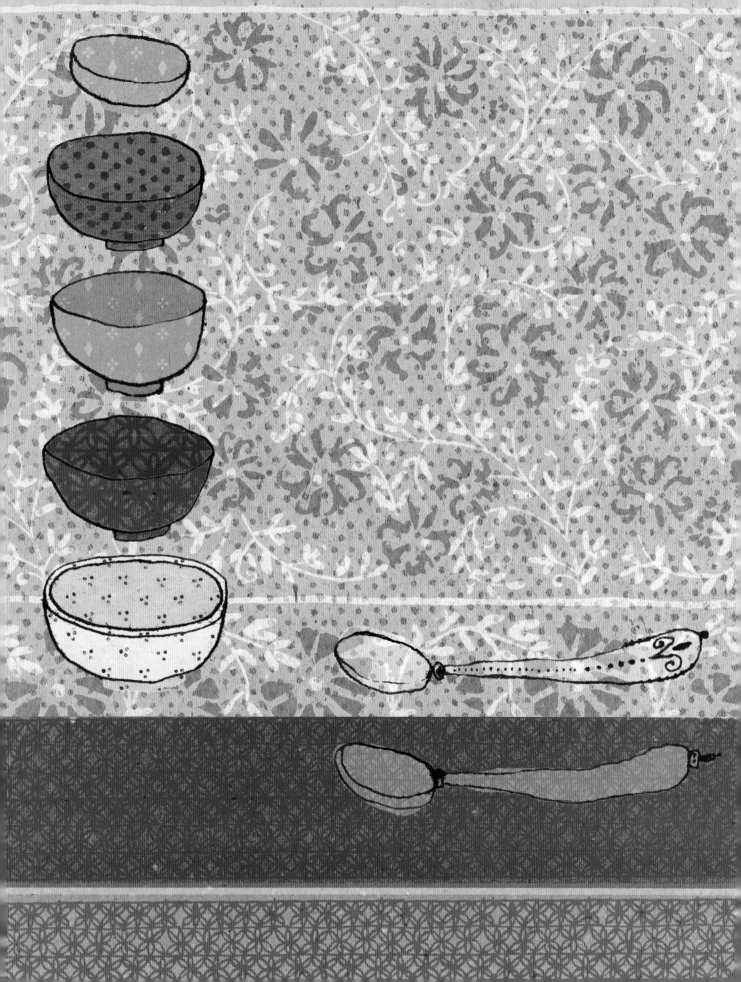

Biriani: A Festive Dish

Rice is cooked in stock and layered with savoury meat or chicken, making this a truly wonderful party dish—a meal in one course. Because this dish consists of three distinct components, each with its mixture of spices, onions, garlic and ginger, I have taken a short cut by using my easy version of Lamb Korma (see note on page 99) for the lamb layer. For an even shorter method, skip making the stock and use some of my Kashmiri Marinade to flavour the rice. It has no chilli in it, and so is mild and fragrant.

Serves 6–8

1 quantity Lamb Korma (see page 98)

Stock
1.5 kg (3 lb) chicken pieces or 3 lamb shanks
½ teaspoon whole black peppercorns
6 green cardamom pods
1 onion, stuck with 5 cloves
2 teaspoons salt or to taste

Spiced Rice
500 g (1 lb) basmati rice
3 tablespoons ghee or oil
2 medium-sized onions, sliced
¼ teaspoon saffron strands or ⅛ teaspoon powdered saffron
2 cloves garlic, crushed
1 teaspoon finely grated ginger
½ teaspoon Garam Masala (see page 168)
½ teaspoon ground cardamom
2 teaspoons salt
¼ cup sultanas

¼ cup fried almonds

To make the Stock, simmer the chicken or lamb in a large pan in enough water to cover with the whole spices, onion and salt for about 2 hours or until a good strong stock results. Strain the stock and reserve. Remove the meat from the bones. Cut the meat into bite-sized pieces and reserve.

Prepare the version of Lamb Korma following the instructions in the note on page 99.

To make the Spiced Rice, wash the rice well and drain in a colander for 1 hour. Heat the ghee in a heavy saucepan with a well-fitting lid. Fry the onions until soft and golden, stirring occasionally.

If using saffron strands, toast them for about a minute in a dry pan, taking care not to let them darken. Turn onto a saucer and when cool and crisp crush them to powder with the back of a spoon. Add 1 tablespoon hot water to dissolve.

Add the garlic and ginger to the onions and fry a minute longer. Add the rice and stir well, then add saffron, 1 litre (2 pints/4 cups) of the hot stock, garam masala, cardamom and salt. When it comes to the boil stir in the sultanas, cover with a well-fitting lid and cook on the lowest heat for 20 minutes. Do not lift lid during this time as it is the steam that cooks the rice.

Turn off the heat, uncover and allow the steam to escape for 10 minutes. The chicken or lamb pieces reserved from the stock can now be added to the rice and gently mixed through.

Transfer one-third of the rice to a buttered ovenproof dish, pressing the layer down lightly. Spread half the lamb korma over the rice, cover with another third of the rice and the remaining lamb. Finally, add a third layer of rice, press down, cover with foil and place in a slow oven, about 150°C (300°F), for 30 minutes.

To serve, garnish the top of the dish with fried almonds or blanched pistachios and serve with accompaniments such as cucumbers in sour cream, chutneys and pappadams.

A short cut to Spiced Rice is to dissolve 2 tablespoons of Charmaine Solomon's Kashmiri Marinade in 1 litre (2 pints/4 cups) hot water and use to cook the rice. Add saffron, salt and sultanas, bring to the boil, cover tightly and cook on low heat for 20 minutes. The onions, garlic, ginger, garam masala and ground cardamom are all in the marinade.

Peas and Fresh Cheese
Mattar Panir

One of India's favourite vegetarian curries. I have found from experience that the best substitute for home-made fresh cheese is baked ricotta. One needs a firm cheese that will not melt when cooked, but hold its shape. If baked ricotta is not sold in your neighbourhood deli, bake it yourself. Buy firm, fresh ricotta (sold by weight in most supermarkets) but allow half as much again, say 750g – 800g, as it loses weight when the moisture evaporates in baking. Cut in 2cm (¾ in) slices and place them on an oven tray lined with baking paper. Bake in a moderate oven, 180°C (350°F) for 30 minutes. Turn slices over and bake a further 20 minutes or until firm and tinged with gold.

Serves 6

500 g (1 lb) baked ricotta
2 tablespoons oil or ghee
2 medium-sized onions, finely chopped
2 cloves garlic, finely chopped
2 teaspoons finely grated fresh ginger
3 teaspoons ground coriander
2 teaspoons ground cumin
1 teaspoon ground turmeric
½ teaspoon chilli powder
2 large ripe tomatoes, peeled and chopped
250 g (8 oz) fresh or frozen peas
1 teaspoon salt or to taste
1 teaspoon Garam Masala (see page 168)
2 tablespoons chopped fresh mint or coriander

Cut the ricotta into slices about 2 cm (¾ in) thick, and then into cubes.

Heat the oil or ghee in a heavy saucepan and fry the onions, garlic and ginger over a medium heat, stirring now and then, until the onion starts to turn golden. Sprinkle in the ground spices and fry, stirring, until the spices darken slightly and smell fragrant.

Add the tomatoes, peas, salt and garam masala. Cover and simmer until the tomatoes are cooked to a pulp and the peas are tender. Frozen peas may be added after the tomatoes are soft, but fresh peas will need longer cooking. If necessary, add a little water if the mixture becomes too dry. Add the cheese and simmer for a further 10 minutes, spooning the spicy tomato gravy over them. Sprinkle with fresh herbs and serve with steamed rice or Kitchri (see page 76).

For ease and speed, heat oil or ghee and fry 3 tablespoons Charmaine Solomon's Butter Chicken Marinade for 2 minutes. Add 250ml (8 fl oz/ 1 cup) tomato purée and 1 tablespoon sugar. Bring to the boil, add 250g (8 oz) frozen peas, thawed. Simmer 5 minutes, add cubes of ricotta and gently heat through. Finally stir in 125ml (4 fl oz/½ cup) cream. Garnish with fresh coriander or mint and serve with rice.

Spicy Potatoes

Serves 4 with rice or chapatis

2 tablespoons ghee or oil
1 teaspoon Panch Phora (see page 170)
1 onion, finely chopped
1 teaspoon turmeric
1 teaspoon ground cumin
½ teaspoon chilli powder
500 g (1 lb) potatoes, peeled and cut into 1 cm (½ in) dice
60 ml (2 fl oz/¼ cup) water
a few sprigs of fresh mint or coriander, chopped
½ teaspoon Garam Masala (see page 168)
½ teaspoon salt or to taste
lemon juice to taste

Heat the ghee or oil in a heavy saucepan and fry the panch phora until the mustard seeds pop. Add the onion and stir over a medium–low heat until soft and starting to colour. Add the ground spices and stir, add the potatoes, mix well and add the water.

Cook on a very low heat, tightly covered, for 20 minutes. Don't lift the lid but shake the pan now and then so the potatoes don't stick. The potatoes should be soft in this time, but test to make sure.

Sprinkle with the chopped herbs, garam masala, salt and lemon juice. If necessary add a couple of tablespoons more water, cover and cook for a few minutes longer. A slight crust may form on the base of the pan, but scrape this up and mix it with the potatoes.

Spicy Stir-fried Cauliflower

Serves 4 as an accompaniment

½ small cauliflower
3 tablespoons oil or ghee
2 teaspoons Panch Phora (see page 170)
2 teaspoons finely chopped garlic
2 teaspoons finely grated ginger
1 teaspoon turmeric
1 teaspoon salt
60 ml (2 fl oz/¼ cup) water
1 teaspoon Garam Masala (see page 168)
2 tablespoons chopped coriander leaves

Slice the cauliflower, keeping some of the stem on each floret.
   Heat the oil or ghee in a wok or deep saucepan and add the panch phora,
frying on medium heat for 1 minute. Add the garlic and ginger
and stir over low heat until the garlic is golden. Add the turmeric and
cauliflower, stirring well. Add salt and water, cover and cook until the
cauliflower is tender but still crisp, about 10 minutes. Sprinkle with
garam masala and coriander.

Chickpea Curry

Serves 4 with rice or flat bread

1 cup dried chickpeas (*kabuli channa*)
2 teaspoons salt
2 tablespoons ghee or oil
2 large onions, finely chopped
2 teaspoons chopped garlic
2 teaspoons finely grated ginger
1 teaspoon turmeric
1 teaspoon Garam Masala (see page 168)
2 large ripe tomatoes, peeled and chopped
1 fresh green chilli, seeded and sliced
2 tablespoons chopped fresh mint or coriander
lemon juice to taste

Soak the chickpeas overnight in enough cold water to cover. Drain, rinse and put the chickpeas with just enough water to cover in a pressure cooker or heavy saucepan. Cook until half tender, then add the salt and cook until done but still holding their shape.

Heat the ghee or oil in a heavy saucepan and fry the onions, garlic and ginger until golden, stirring frequently. Add the turmeric and fry for a few seconds, then add the garam masala, tomatoes, chilli and half the chopped mint or coriander. Add the chickpeas and their cooking liquid, stir, cover and simmer on low heat until the chickpeas are very tender and the tomatoes have cooked to a purée. Add lemon juice to taste and sprinkle with the remaining fresh herbs.

Samosas

I long ago stopped making pastry to enclose samosas, since frozen spring roll wrappers available in supermarkets are such a good substitute.

Makes 36

2 tablespoons ghee or oil
1 teaspoon finely chopped garlic
1 teaspoon finely chopped ginger
2 medium-sized onions, finely chopped
2 teaspoons curry powder
½ teaspoon salt
1 tablespoon lemon juice
250 (8 oz) minced lamb or beef
60 ml (2 fl oz/¼ cup) hot water
1 teaspoon Garam Masala (see page 168)
2 tablespoons chopped fresh mint or coriander
12 sheets spring roll pastry, 215 mm (8 in) square
oil for frying

Heat the ghee or oil in a saucepan and on gentle heat fry the garlic, ginger and half the chopped onions until the onion is soft. Add curry powder, salt and lemon juice. Add the mince and fry over high heat until the meat is no longer pink. Add hot water, lower the heat, cover and cook until the meat is tender and all the liquid has been absorbed. Turn off the heat and allow the filling to cool. Sprinkle with garam masala, chopped herbs and the remaining onion and mix through.

Allow the spring roll pastry to thaw while preparing the filling. Separate 12 sheets, return the rest to the packet and freeze. With a sharp knife cut the square into 3 equal strips. Put a spoonful of filling at one end and fold one corner of the pastry over diagonally. Fold again, still keeping a triangular shape and lining up the edges so that the filling is completely enclosed. Moisten the end of the strip with water or a mixture of flour and water and press lightly to seal.

Heat the oil in a deep pan (a wok is ideal) and when very hot, fry no more than about 5 at a time, turning, until golden brown all over. Lift out on a slotted spoon and drain on absorbent paper. Serve warm or at room temperature. Serve with Mint Chutney (see page 88).

Vegetable Samosas
Peel 2 large potatoes and cut into 1 cm (¾ in) dice. Drop into boiling salted water with 1 teaspoon turmeric and cook until the potato is soft but still holds its shape. Drain, sprinkle with 1 teaspoon ground cumin, ½ teaspoon Garam Masala (see page 168) and 2 tablespoons lemon juice. Allow to cool and mix in 1 finely chopped onion. Proceed as for meat samosas.

87

Chutneys, Sambals and Raitas

Mint or Coriander Chutney

A great dip for Samosas (see page 87).

1 cup firmly packed mint or coriander leaves
6 spring onions, chopped
2 fresh green chillies, sliced
1 teaspoon salt
2 teaspoons sugar
1 teaspoon Garam Masala (see page 168)
4 tablespoons lemon juice
2 tablespoons water

Blend all ingredients to a purée. Serve as is, or mix with a little natural yoghurt if a lighter dip is preferred.

Coconut and Herb Chutney

1 cup desiccated or freshly grated coconut
4 spring onions or 1 medium onion, chopped
½ cup lime or lemon juice
½ cup mint or coriander leaves
1 teaspoon salt
1 teaspoon ghee or oil
2 teaspoons black mustard seeds
2 teaspoons cumin seeds

If using desiccated coconut put into a bowl and sprinkle with 3 tablespoons water or sufficient to moisten all the coconut. Put the onions, lime or lemon juice and fresh herbs into the blender and liquidise. Add salt and coconut and blend again to make a thick puree.

Heat ghee or oil in a small pan and fry the mustard and cumin seeds, stirring, until mustard seeds pop. Pour over the coconut mixture and mix with a spoon. Serve in a small dish as an accompaniment.

88

Cucumber Raita

1 clove garlic
½ teaspoon salt
250 ml (8 fl oz/1 cup) natural yoghurt
125 ml (4 fl oz/½ cup) light sour cream
1 teaspoon finely grated fresh ginger
2 teaspoons finely shredded mint leaves
1 seedless cucumber, finely sliced

Crush the garlic with the salt using the flat of a knife on a wooden board, until a smooth paste forms. In a bowl mix together the yoghurt, sour cream, ginger, garlic and mint leaves. Finally stir in the cucumber. Serve chilled, as an accompaniment to a hot curry.

Banana Raita

2 tablespoons lemon juice
2 teaspoons sugar
½ teaspoon salt
a good pinch of chilli powder
1 teaspoon ghee or oil
1 teaspoon cumin seeds
1 teaspoon black mustard seeds
375 ml (12 fl oz/1½ cups) natural yoghurt
2 cups sliced bananas (about 3 large ripe bananas)

Stir together the lemon juice, sugar, salt and chilli powder.
    Heat the ghee or oil and fry the cumin and black mustard seeds. When the mustard seeds pop, pour over the yoghurt and mix. Fold in the bananas and the lemon juice mixture. If liked, 3 tablespoons freshly grated coconut or desiccated coconut may be added to the raita. Serve with rice and curries.

Onion Sambal

2 small onions, finely sliced
2 tablespoons lemon or lime juice
½ teaspoon salt
½ teaspoon chilli powder

Toss all the ingredients together in a bowl until well mixed. Serve with a curry meal or with Tandoori-style Chicken (see page 95).

Coconut Sambal
A favourite in Sri Lanka.

2 cups grated fresh coconut
1 scant teaspoon salt
1 scant teaspoon chilli powder
2 teaspoons paprika
1 medium-sized onion, finely chopped
2 tablespoons lime or lemon juice
2 teaspoons maldive fish, finely pounded (if available)

Combine all the ingredients. For seasoned chilli eaters the amount of chilli powder may be increased. Mix well. Add finely pounded maldive fish if using. Serve with rice and curries.

Chilli and Dried Prawn Sambal
A popular accompaniment to rice and curry meals in Sri Lanka.

½ cup vegetable oil
4 medium onions, finely sliced
2 teaspoons chilli powder or to taste
60g (2 oz) dried shrimp or maldive fish, ground in blender
    or 1 x 160g (5 ½ oz) can 'minced prawns in spices'
3 tablespoons tamarind pulp
3 tablespoons water
½ teaspoon salt
1 tablespoon sugar

Heat oil in heavy frying pan and fry onions on low heat, stirring now and then, until soft and transparent. When onion is golden brown add chilli powder and the dried shrimp or maldive fish, or canned prawns in spices. Add tamarind pulp, water and salt. Stir well, cover and simmer 15 minutes. Uncover and cook until liquid evaporates and mixture is thick. Stir in sugar and cool. Store in a glass jar and use in small quantities as a relish.

NOTE: Maldive fish is a type of bonito which is cured and sundried until very hard. It keeps indefinitely and is pounded into small fragments which are an important flavouring in Sri Lankan dishes.

Spicy Scrambled Eggs, Parsi Style

Serves 4

6 eggs
60 ml (2 fl oz/¼ cup) milk
½ teaspoon salt or to taste
¼ teaspoon ground black pepper
2 tablespoons ghee or butter
6 spring onions, finely chopped
2–3 fresh green or red chillies, seeded and chopped
1 teaspoon finely grated ginger
a big pinch of turmeric
3 tablespoons chopped fresh coriander
1 ripe tomato, finely diced (optional)
½ teaspoon ground cumin
tomato wedges (optional)
fresh coriander sprigs (optional)

Beat the eggs until well mixed. Stir in the milk, salt and pepper.

Heat the ghee or butter in a large frying pan and cook the spring onions, chillies and ginger until soft. Add the turmeric, coriander, diced tomato, if using, and cumin and fry for 1–2 minutes, then stir in the egg mixture. Cook over a low heat, stirring and lifting the eggs as they set on the bottom of the pan, stopping when the mixture is still of a creamy consistency. Turn onto a serving plate and garnish, if liked, with tomato wedges and sprigs of fresh coriander. Delicious with freshly cooked chapatis or puris, but equally good on freshly made hot toast.

Fish with Green Chutney
Patrani Machchi

Fillets of fish are coated with green chutney and wrapped in banana leaves before cooking. Served in the banana leaf parcel, it is featured at Parsi weddings and is an impressive way to serve fish at a dinner party.

Serves 6

1 kg (2 lb) boneless fillets of firm white fish
salt
2 tablespoons ghee or oil
banana leaves cut into large squares
lime wedges

Green Chutney
juice of 2 limes or 1 lemon
½ cup chopped onion
2 cups chopped fresh coriander leaves
½ cup chopped fresh mint
4 large green chillies, seeded and chopped
3 cloves garlic, peeled and chopped
½ teaspoon ground cumin
1 cup grated fresh coconut or ¼ cup desiccated coconut
2 tablespoons ghee or oil
1 teaspoon salt
1 teaspoon Garam Masala (see page 168)

Wash the fish fillets and dry on kitchen paper, then sprinkle lightly with salt and cut into serving pieces. Set aside while preparing the chutney.

To make the Green Chutney, put all the ingredients into a blender. It helps if the onions and lime juice go in first, since the blades need liquid to draw the ingredients down. Add a little water if necessary and blend to a purée, but do not make the purée too wet. (If using desiccated coconut, first moisten by sprinkling with a little water and mix lightly with fingertips.)

Fry the green chutney on low heat in ghee or oil until fragrant. When cool, spread on both sides of the fish fillet pieces.

To prevent the banana leaf splitting, pass it over a gas flame or put it under an electric grill until it becomes pliable. Wrap each serving of fish securely in a piece of banana leaf, fasten with wooden toothpicks and steam over gently simmering water for 30 minutes.

Or the banana-leaf parcels can be shallow-fried in just enough oil to cover the base of a heavy frying pan. Allow about 7 minutes for each side, depending on the thickness of the fish.

Serve with lime wedges. Diners unwrap the banana leaf before eating.

Spicy Clams

If clams are not available, use mussels. Discard any mussels that are not tightly closed when purchased, and any that do not open during cooking.

Serves 4

1 kg (2 lb) clams or mussels
3 tablespoons ghee or oil
2 large onions, finely chopped
3 cloves garlic, finely chopped
3 teaspoons finely chopped fresh ginger
3 fresh red chillies, seeded and chopped
½ teaspoon ground turmeric
3 teaspoons ground coriander
½ teaspoon salt
250 ml (8 fl oz/1 cup) water
1 tablespoon chopped fresh coriander leaves
lime or lemon juice to taste

Swish the clams in water to lose any sand they may have retained. If using mussels, scrub and beard them.

Heat the ghee in a large, deep pan and fry the onions, garlic and ginger on medium heat until the onions are soft and golden. Add the chillies, turmeric, coriander and stir for a few minutes. Add salt and water and bring to the boil. Cover the pan and simmer for 5 minutes. Add the clams or mussels, cover and steam for 10 minutes or until the shells have opened. Remove from the heat and sprinkle in the coriander. Add extra salt if required, and a good squeeze of lime or lemon juice. Spoon the spicy sauce over and serve at once with steamed rice.

Tandoori-style Chicken

In Indian restaurants the chicken comes out bright orange-red. No artificial colouring is used in my recipe.

Serves 4

2 spatchcock, about 500 g (1 lb) each
2 tablespoons ghee (if cooking in oven)

Marinade
175 ml (6 fl oz/¾ cup) natural yoghurt
1½ teaspoons salt
1½ teaspoons crushed garlic
1½ teaspoons finely grated ginger
½ teaspoon white pepper
½ teaspoon chilli powder
1 teaspoon Garam Masala (page 168)
¼ teaspoon ground fenugreek seeds
½ teaspoon ground fenugreek leaves
3 teaspoons paprika
2 teaspoons ground coriander
1 teaspoon ground cumin
juice of 1 lime

With a sharp knife cut through the skin of the chicken right down the centre, front and back. Skin the chickens, then make slits in the flesh to allow the spices to penetrate.

To make the Marinade, combine the yoghurt with all the other ingredients. Rub the marinade all over as well as inside the chickens and leave for 2 hours or cover and refrigerate overnight.

A barbecue with a cover is the next best thing to a *tandoor*, which is a clay oven heated by charcoal. Make sure the fire has burned down to glowing coals. Place the chickens on a rack above the coals and cook until tender, turning them so they cook on all sides. If more convenient for your kind of barbecue, cut the chickens in half lengthways before cooking.

They may also be cooked in a hot oven at 200°C (400°F). Melt the ghee in a roasting pan, put the 2 chickens in the pan, side by side, breasts downwards. Brush with the melted ghee and roast for 20 minutes. Turn the chickens on one side and roast for another 15 minutes, then turn them on the other side and roast for a further 15 minutes. For the final 10 minutes turn them breast upwards and baste after 5 minutes. If your barbecue or oven has a rotisserie they may be roasted on this, but remember to baste as the skin has been removed. Serve hot with parathas or naan and Onion Sambal (see page 89).

95

You can use my bottled Tandoori Tikka Marinade, which contains all the Marinade ingredients listed above except yoghurt.

Saffron Chicken

Simple to prepare and with such superb flavour, this is one of my favourite chicken dishes. It is typical of North Indian cooking. Be sure you purchase the saffron from a reputable supplier, since there are many yellow powders and bright orange strands labelled saffron which are not. Some cooks soak the saffron strands in hot milk or hot water and add them whole, but I think the method I have described below diffuses the flavour more evenly.

Serves 4–5

1.5 kg (3 lb) roasting chicken
3 tablespoons ghee
1 large onion, finely chopped
2 teaspoons finely chopped garlic
1 teaspoon finely grated ginger
3 fresh red chillies, seeded and sliced
½ teaspoon saffron strands or ¼ teaspoon ground saffron
½ teaspoon ground cardamom
1½ teaspoons salt or to taste

Cut the chicken into small serving pieces: divide the breast into quarters, separate thighs from drumsticks and disjoint the wings.

Heat the ghee in a heavy saucepan and cook the onion, garlic, ginger and chillies on low heat, stirring frequently, until the onion starts to turn golden.

Heat the saffron strands in a small dry pan for about 1 minute, shaking the pan or stirring so that they don't darken. Turn onto a saucer to cool and crisp, then crush with the back of a spoon. Dissolve in 1 tablespoon boiling water. Add to the pan with the cardamom and stir well, then add the chicken pieces. Turn the chicken pieces for 5 minutes or until each is coated with the saffron mixture. Add salt, cover and cook over moderate heat for 15 minutes or until the chicken is tender. Uncover the pan and continue cooking until most of the liquid evaporates. Serve with parathas or rice.

Butter Chicken
Murgh Makhani

For this dish, you're supposed to first prepare tandoori chicken and make sure there is enough left over for this equally popular chicken cooked in a saffron-scented creamy sauce. This is a simple method and just as good.

Serves 6 with rice

Marinade
2 tablespoons natural yoghurt
3 teaspoons salt
3 teaspoons crushed garlic
3 teaspoons finely grated ginger
1 teaspoon white pepper
1 teaspoon chilli powder
2 teaspoons Garam Masala (page 168)
½ teaspoon ground fenugreek seeds
1½ tablespoons paprika
1 tablespoon ground coriander
2 teaspoons ground cumin
juice of 1 lime
½ teaspoon saffron strands or ¼ teaspoon saffron powder

6 chicken thigh cutlets (bone in, skin on) or 750 g (1½ lb) thigh fillets, diced
3 tablespoons ghee or butter
4 tomatoes, peeled and chopped, or 250 ml (8 fl oz/1 cup) tomato purée
2 teaspoons sugar
125 ml (4 fl oz/½ cup) cream
fresh coriander sprigs

To make the Marinade, combine all the ingredients.

Rub over the chicken thighs or fillets. Cover and leave for at least 30 minutes.

Heat the ghee in a heavy frying pan and brown the joints on both sides, or fry the diced chicken till no longer pink. Add the tomatoes or tomato purée, cover and simmer until the chicken is cooked through. Add sugar and cream and stir well. Serve garnished with sprigs of fresh coriander.

Make double or triple quantities of the Marinade and keep it in the refrigerator for up to a month, or use Charmaine Solomon's Butter Chicken Marinade, which contains all the ingredients you'll need. Either way, use 4 tablespoons for 6 thigh cutlets or 3 tablespoons for 750 g diced fillets. Proceed from the second line of the method.

Lamb Korma

Here we have the traditional recipe, which is fairly labour intensive if you make it from start to finish. A much easier modern way to achieve the same result is to make the Korma Paste beforehand and store it in the refrigerator in a clean glass jar, or to use my Charmaine Solomon's Korma Curry Paste. You save so much preparation time that this recipe becomes easy Lamb Korma. The details of this alternative method appear on page 99.

Once it is cooked, this dish improves with keeping (in the refrigerator), and so is ideal for preparing ahead. It is delicious in its own right, sprinkled with fresh coriander leaves just before serving. It is also the savoury lamb for Biriyani (see page 80).

A photograph of this dish appears on page 101.

Serves 6 with rice or roti

Korma Paste
2 medium-sized onions
1 tablespoon chopped fresh ginger
4 cloves garlic
¼ cup blanched almonds or raw cashews
2 dried red chillies, stems and seeds removed
125 ml (4 fl oz/½ cup) water
2 teaspoons ground coriander
1 teaspoon ground cumin
¼ teaspoon ground cinnamon
¼ teaspoon ground cardamom
¼ teaspoon ground cloves
¼ teaspoon ground mace or nutmeg
½ teaspoon saffron strands or ⅛ teaspoon saffron powder
2 tablespoons boiling water
1 tablespoon ghee
2 tablespoons vegetable oil
60 ml (2 fl oz/¼ cup) water
2 teaspoons salt or to taste

1 kg (2 lb) lamb leg or chump chops, bone left in
2–3 ripe tomatoes, peeled, seeded and chopped
125 ml (4 fl oz/½ cup) natural yoghurt
125 ml (4 fl oz/½ cup) cream
2 tablespoons chopped coriander

Make the Korma Paste as follows.

Peel the onions, slice one finely and set aside. Chop the remaining onion and put in a blender with the ginger, garlic, almonds or cashews and chillis. Add 125ml (4 fl oz/½ cup) water to the blender, cover and blend on high speed to form a smooth puree. Add the ground spices and blend.

If using saffron strands, toast them lightly in a dry pan for less than a minute – they should not darken. Turn onto a saucer to cool and crisp, then crush to powder with the back of a spoon. Dissolve in boiling water. Add to blender and combine again.

Heat the ghee and oil in a large saucepan and when hot put in the reserved sliced onion. Fry, stirring frequently with a wooden spoon, until soft and golden. Add the blended mixture and continue to fry, stirring constantly until the purée is well cooked and the oil starts to separate from the mixture. Rinse the blender with extra 60ml (2 fl oz/¼ cup) water, add to the pan with salt and fry until the liquid is thick and dry.

If you are not making the Lamb Korma immediately, store this paste in a clean dry glass jar in the refrigerator.

Cut the lamb chops into pieces and trim off any excess fat. Add the lamb to the hot Korma Paste and stir over a medium heat until each cube is coated with spice. Add the tomatoes, cover and cook until the meat is tender. Combine yoghurt and cream and add to the pan. Stir to ensure the spices don't stick to the base of the pan. The sauce should be very thick and smooth. Sprinkle with fresh coriander.

Make the easy version of Lamb Korma, by making double or triple quantities of the Korma Paste and keeping it in the refrigerator. You can also use Charmaine Solomon's Korma Curry Paste. For 1 kg (2 lb) lamb forequarter chump chops (bone left in, cubed) use 4 tablespoons Korma Paste. Heat 2 tablespoons of ghee or oil in a heavy saucepan and fry the meat until brown, turning so it cooks evenly. Add 300g (10 oz) tomato purée or ripe tomatoes (peeled, seeded and chopped) and cook until tender, adding a little water from time to time if necessary. When the meat is soft, and the tomatoes cooked to a purée, combine 125 ml (4 fl oz/½ cup) yoghurt with 125 ml (4 fl oz/½ cup) cream and stir into the korma. Cook uncovered until the gravy is thick and coats the lamb.

Sprinkle with fresh coriander leaves just before serving.

NOTE: The Korma Paste on page 98, and Charmaine Solomon's Korma Curry Paste are both concentrates, not sauces. Please do not substitute another product and expect the same results.

Kofta Curry

One of my favourite Indian dishes, since there is so much flavour in every bite. Minced lamb is combined with onion, garlic, ginger, chillies and fresh coriander or mint, formed into koftas (balls), browned and simmered in a spicy gravy that echoes similar flavours.

Serves 6 with rice

Meatballs
750 g (1½ lb) minced lamb
1 large onion, finely chopped
1 clove garlic, crushed
1½ teaspoons salt
1 teaspoon finely grated ginger
1 fresh red or green chilli, seeded and finely chopped
3 tablespoons finely chopped mint or coriander
1 teaspoon Garam Masala (see page 168)

Gravy
3 tablespoons ghee or oil
2 medium-sized onions, finely chopped
2 cloves garlic, finely chopped
1 tablespoon finely chopped fresh ginger
1 teaspoon ground turmeric
1 teaspoon Garam Masala (see page 168)
1 teaspoon chilli powder or to taste
2 large ripe tomatoes, peeled and finely chopped
1 teaspoon salt
2 tablespoons chopped coriander or mint
lemon juice to taste

To make the Meatballs, mix the lamb thoroughly with all the other ingredients. Shape into small balls.

To make the Gravy, heat the ghee or oil in a large, heavy saucepan. Brown the meatballs, remove from the pan and set aside. In the same pan fry the onions, garlic and ginger until soft and golden. Add turmeric, garam masala and chilli powder. Fry for 1 minute. Add tomatoes, salt and meatballs, cover and simmer for 25 minutes or until the gravy is thick. Stir in the chopped herbs and lemon juice.

100

Opposite page: Lamb Korma (see page 98)

Roast Leg of Lamb Kashmiri Style
Raan

This is an easy dish, but so effective.

Serves 8

1 x 2.5 kg (5 lb) leg of lamb

Marinade
5 cloves garlic
3 level teaspoons salt
1 tablespoon finely grated ginger
1 teaspoon ground cumin
1 teaspoon ground turmeric
½ teaspoon ground black pepper
½ teaspoon ground cinnamon
½ teaspoon ground cardamom
¼ teaspoon ground cloves
2 tablespoons lemon juice

½ teaspoon saffron strands or ¼ teaspoon powdered saffron
250 ml (8 fl oz/1 cup) natural yoghurt
2 tablespoons blanched almonds
2 tablespoons blanched pistachios
1 tablespoon honey

Remove the skin and any excess fat from the lamb. With the point of a small knife make deep slits all over the lamb.

To make the Marinade, crush the garlic with salt to form a smooth paste. Combine with the ginger, ground spices and lemon juice.

Rub the marinade over the lamb and press some into each slit. Put the lamb in a deep bowl. If using saffron strands, toast them lightly for less than a minute in a dry pan over low heat, just long enough to dry them. Turn onto a saucer and leave to cool and crisp, then crush to powder with the back of a spoon. Dissolve the powder in 1 tablespoon hot water.

Put yoghurt, saffron, almonds and pistachios into a blender and process until smooth. Spoon the mixture over the lamb. Drizzle the honey over, cover the bowl with plastic wrap and leave to marinate at least overnight in the refrigerator, or 2 days if possible.

Preheat the oven to very hot, 230°C (450°F). Transfer the lamb to a baking dish with a cover and roast in the oven for 30 minutes, then reduce the heat to 180°C (350°F) and cook for a further 1 hour 45 minutes or until the lamb is cooked through. Uncover the baking dish and cool to room temperature. Serve with rice or flat bread. Leftovers make superb sandwiches.

If short on time, a quick solution is to buy a boned and butterflied leg of lamb, spread it with 2–3 tablespoons Charmaine Solomon's Kashmiri Marinade and leave at room temperature for 30 minutes, then cook on a barbecue or in the oven for about 35 minutes.

Goan Pork Vindaloo

This is a cross between a curry and a pickle, and high in acidity. Cook it in a non-reactive pan. In India this would be an earthenware pot, but enamel or heavy stainless steel would be a suitable substitute.

Serves 8

8–10 large dried red chillies
2 tablespoons black mustard seeds
250 ml (8 fl oz/1 cup) coconut vinegar or white vinegar
10–15 cloves garlic, peeled
5 cm (2 in) piece of fresh ginger, roughly chopped
1 kg (2 lb) pork, cut into large cubes
1 tablespoon ground cumin
½ teaspoon ground black pepper
½ teaspoon ground cinnamon
½ teaspoon ground cardamom
½ teaspoon ground cloves
½ teaspoon ground nutmeg
2 teaspoons salt
3 tablespoons ghee or oil
2 medium-sized onions, finely chopped
1 tablespoon brown sugar

Break the stems off the chillies and shake out the seeds. Soak the chillies and mustard seeds in vinegar overnight. Put into a blender with the garlic and ginger. Blend to a purée.

Place the pork in a china bowl and add the blended mixture, ground spices and salt. Mix thoroughly so all the pieces of pork are coated, and marinate for 2 hours.

Heat the ghee or oil and fry the onions on low heat until soft and golden, stirring frequently, about 20 minutes. When the oil separates from the onions, drain the pieces of pork from the marinade and brown them in the pan. Pour in the marinade, cover and simmer on low heat until the pork is tender. Stir in the sugar and serve with steamed rice and vegetable accompaniments.

Sri Lanka-style Lentils

Featuring the same main ingredient as the recipe for dhal, but the result is sufficiently different and worth a try so you can decide which is your favourite. Instead of water, coconut milk is the cooking medium. The flavours are different because distinctively flavoured ingredients are added to the frying onions and cooked along with the lentils.

Serves 6

250 g (8 oz) red lentils
2 tablespoons ghee or oil
2 large onions, finely sliced
2 cloves garlic, chopped
1 teaspoon finely grated fresh ginger
1 teaspoon ground turmeric
750 ml (24 fl oz/3 cups) thin coconut milk
2 teaspoons pounded maldive fish
1–2 dried chillies
a sprig of curry leaves
5 cm (2 in) strip of pandan leaf
1 stem lemongrass, bruised
1 cinnamon quill
1 teaspoon salt
125 ml (4 fl oz/½ cup) thick coconut milk

Wash the lentils well in several changes of cold water, discarding any that float. Drain the lentils in a sieve.

In a heavy saucepan heat the ghee and fry the onions until golden brown. Remove half the onions and set aside for garnish. Add the garlic and ginger and fry a few seconds longer. Add the turmeric and stir, then add the lentils and stir for a couple of minutes. Add the thin coconut milk and remaining ingredients except the salt and thick coconut milk. Bring to the boil. Lower the heat, cover and simmer for 20 minutes or until the lentils are half cooked. Add the salt, mix well and cook until the lentils are soft and puréed. If the mixture is too liquid, cook uncovered to evaporate some of the water. After cooking add the thick coconut milk. This lentil dish should have a rather wet consistency. Serve garnished with the reserved fried onions.

Ghee Rice

Each country has its own special method of cooking rice. In North India, the most prized rice is basmati, a fragrant, long-grain rice that is cooked on its own (*namkin chawal*), or with lentils (*kitchri*), or in spicy stock (*yakhni pilau*). It is always cooked by the absorption method. If basmati rice is not available, use any long-grain rice. The most important point to watch is the proportion of rice to liquid. Use the same size measuring cups for both rice and liquid, and the result will be perfectly cooked rice every time.

In Sri Lanka, basmati rice is not as readily available as it is in India or even in western countries. If available, it is very expensive. So this dish would most likely feature *muttu samba* (translates as 'pearl samba') a tiny, round grain that, like basmati, offers the quality of fluffy, separate rice.

Serves 4–6

500 g (1 lb/2 ½ cups) basmati or other long grain rice
2 tablespoons ghee or oil
1 onion, finely sliced
1 cinnamon quill
6 green cardamom pods, bruised
6 whole cloves
1 litre (2 pints/4 cups) hot stock or water
2 teaspoons salt (if stock is unsalted)

Wash the rice well and drain in a sieve for about 30 minutes.

Heat the ghee or oil in a heavy saucepan and fry the onion until golden brown. Add the spices and well-drained rice, stirring with a slotted metal spoon, about 3 minutes or until all the grains are coated with ghee.

Add the hot stock and salt, and bring quickly to the boil. Cover the pan with a tight-fitting lid and turn the heat as low as possible. Cook for 15–20 minutes without lifting the lid or stirring. Turn off the heat and leave covered for a further 5 minutes. Then remove the lid to allow steam to escape for a few minutes and fluff the rice with a fork. Remove the whole spices.

The rice may be kept warm in the same pot, covered, for 1 hour. Serve with a metal spoon that won't crush the grains.

If using a rice cooker, there are a few things to consider. Some brands say you can fry the spices on 'cook' mode, so fry the onions, spices and rice as per the saucepan method. If the pan has a non-stick surface, there is the likelihood of scratching it, so be sure to use a wooden or plastic spoon to stir. Read the instructions carefully and don't do anything you're not supposed to—it may invalidate your appliance guarantee.

NOTE: For plain steamed rice omit the ghee, onion and spices. Use hot water rather than stock.

Sri Lanka Prawn Curry

A spicy dish based on coconut milk, chillies and spices, the flavours of this curry will be familiar to those who have experienced Sri Lankan and South Indian food.

Serves 6 with steamed rice

1 kg (2 lb) raw prawns in their shells
6 large dried red chillies
2 medium-sized onions, chopped
3 large cloves garlic, chopped
3 teaspoons finely chopped fresh ginger
3 tablespoons oil
a sprig of fresh curry leaves or 12 dried leaves
1 teaspoon ground turmeric
1 teaspoon ground coriander
1 teaspoon ground cumin
½ teaspoon ground fennel
2 teaspoons paprika
2 teaspoons salt
1 stem lemongrass, bruised
1 strip pandan leaf, about 10 cm (4 in) long
1 x 400 ml (13 fl oz) can coconut milk
lemon juice to taste

Wash the prawns and remove the hard shell from head but leave the legs and body shell on. In Sri Lanka and India, prawns are often cooked in their shells for better flavour.

Soak the chillies in hot water for 15 minutes, then put into a blender with some of the soaking water and the onions, garlic and ginger. Blend to a purée.

Heat the oil and fry the curry leaves for 30 seconds, then add the puréed mixture and the ground spices. Fry, stirring, until the mixture develops a good aroma. Add the salt, lemongrass, pandan leaf and coconut milk and stir while bringing to a slow boil. Do not cover. Simmer for 10 minutes, then add the prawns and simmer uncovered for 10 minutes longer or until the prawns are cooked. Taste and add lemon juice to give a piquant flavour.

Fish Molee

Seafood cooked in mildly seasoned coconut milk has to be the comfort food of those who grew up in South India or its neighbouring island of Sri Lanka. Ideal for those who enjoy flavour but don't like their food hot or pungent. Serve a coconut sambal alongside for those who need a chilli fix.

Serves 4–6

750 g (1½ lb) firm fish steaks
lemon juice
1 teaspoon ground turmeric
1 teaspoon salt
2 tablespoons oil or ghee
2 small onions, thinly sliced
3 cloves garlic, sliced
3 slices fresh ginger, cut into slivers
a large sprig of fresh curry leaves
2 fresh green chillies
500 ml (16 fl oz/2 cups) thin coconut milk
125 ml (4 fl oz/½ cup) thick coconut milk
lime juice and salt to taste

Wipe fish steaks with a damp kitchen towel. Sprinkle with lemon juice, turmeric and salt.

Heat the oil or ghee in a saucepan and on low heat fry the onions, garlic, ginger, curry leaves and chillies until the onions are soft. Stir frequently and do not let the ingredients brown. Add the thin coconut milk (dilute canned coconut milk with an equal amount of water) and stir while it comes to a simmer. Add the fish and cook slowly, uncovered, for 10 minutes. Add the thick (undiluted) coconut milk, stir gently until heated through and remove from the heat. Add lime juice and salt to taste. Serve with steamed rice.

Country Captain

Gentle spicing adds interest to a pot roast and obviously was inspired by the efforts of native cooks to please their western masters. The name, however, is strange indeed. It is thought it came from the cooks' efforts to say 'capon' and, of course, anything cooked with local flavours was described as 'country'. This dish turns up in India, Sri Lanka, Malaysia and wherever the British colonised.

Serves 6

1.5 kg (3 lb) roasting chicken or chicken joints
2 large cloves garlic
2 teaspoons salt
2 teaspoons finely grated fresh ginger
1 teaspoon turmeric
½ teaspoon freshly ground black pepper
a pinch of chilli powder (optional)
1 tablespoon lime juice
3 tablespoons ghee (or a mixture of ghee and oil)
4 large onions, thinly sliced
2 fresh red chillies, seeded and sliced

If using a whole chicken, remove excess fat from the cavity.

With the flat of a knife on a wooden board, crush the garlic with salt to a smooth purée. Mix with the ginger, turmeric, pepper, chilli powder and lime juice. With a sharp skewer prick the skin of the chicken all over and rub with the mixture. Set aside for 30 minutes, or place in a bowl, cover with plastic wrap and refrigerate for longer. Do the same if using chicken joints.

Heat the ghee in a heavy pan and fry half the onions, stirring frequently, until a deep golden brown. Set aside for garnishing the chicken. Fry the remaining onions and chillies until the onions are lightly browned, adding more ghee or oil as necessary. Add the chicken and fry until golden, turning with tongs to brown all over. Add a little water (about 60 ml/2 fl oz/¼ cup) to the pan, cover and cook over low heat until the chicken is tender. At end of cooking, uncover the pan and allow the liquid to evaporate. Serve hot, accompanied by Ghee Rice (see page 106) and garnished with the browned onions. It goes equally well with parboiled and pan-fried potatoes.

Sri Lanka Chicken Curry

Serves 6

1.5 kg (3 lb) roasting chicken or chicken pieces

Spice Mixture
3 tablespoons oil
¼ teaspoon fenugreek seeds
a sprig of fresh curry leaves
2 large onions, finely chopped
3 teaspoons chopped garlic
3 teaspoons finely grated ginger
1 teaspoon turmeric
1 teaspoon chilli powder
1 tablespoon ground coriander
2 teaspoons ground cumin
1 teaspoon ground fennel
2 teaspoons paprika
2 teaspoons salt
2 tablespoons vinegar or lemon juice
2 tomatoes, peeled and chopped
6 cardamom pods, bruised
1 cinnamon quill

1 stem lemongrass, whole, bruised
250 ml (8 fl oz/1 cup) thick coconut milk

Cut the chicken into 'curry' pieces, which means cutting breast and thighs in half, leaving the wings and drumsticks whole.

Heat the oil and fry the fenugreek seeds and curry leaves until they start to brown. Add the onions, garlic and ginger and fry on a medium–low heat until the onions are soft and golden. Add the turmeric, chilli powder, coriander, cumin, fennel, paprika, salt and vinegar. Stir well.

Add the chicken pieces and stir over a medium heat until the pieces are thoroughly coated with spices. Add the tomatoes, whole spices and lemongrass, leaves tied in a knot. Cover and cook on low heat for about 45 minutes. Add the coconut milk, leave the pan uncovered, and taste and correct the seasoning with salt and a little lemon juice if desired. Remove the lemongrass and serve with Ghee Rice (see page 106) and accompaniments.

A quicker way to make this is to use Charmaine Solomon's Sri Lanka Curry Paste instead of the Spice Mixture ingredients. There is no need to chop onions, garlic and ginger, as they are already in the paste. Even curry leaves have been added, but if you wanted to add a sprig of these or a short length of pandan leaf or a stem of lemongrass, all the better.

Dry-fried Pork Curry

In this dish, the pork fries in its own fat. Delicious, but not to be indulged too often.

Serves 6–8

1 tablespoon tamarind pulp
300 ml (10 fl oz) hot water
1 kg (2 lb) pork belly or meaty spareribs, not too lean
3 tablespoons oil

200 ml (7 fl oz) canned coconut milk

Spices
a sprig of fresh curry leaves
½ teaspoon fenugreek seeds
2 large onions, finely chopped
5 cloves garlic, finely chopped
2.5 cm (1 in) piece fresh ginger, finely chopped or grated
4 tablespoons Sri Lanka Curry Powder (see page 169)
2 teaspoons chilli powder or to taste
2 teaspoons salt
1 tablespoon vinegar
1 cinnamon quill
5 cardamom pods, bruised

Soak the tamarind pulp in the hot water until cool enough to handle. Squeeze until all the pulp is dissolved. Strain through a nylon sieve. Discard the seeds and fibres and reserve the liquid.

Cut the pork into large cubes, keeping any skin and fat on.

Heat the oil in a heavy saucepan and fry the curry leaves and fenugreek seeds, stirring, until they start to brown. Add the onions and garlic and fry over a low heat until onion is soft and golden. Add the ginger, curry powder, chilli powder, salt and vinegar and mix well. Add the pork and fry on high heat, stirring frequently, until the pork is coated with the spice mixture. Pour in the tamarind liquid. Add the cinnamon and cardamom. Cover the pan and cook on gentle heat until the pork is tender, about 1 hour. Add the coconut milk and simmer uncovered for 10 minutes.

Pour the gravy into another pan, return the first pan with the pork to the heat and allow to fry in its own fat, stirring and turning the pieces until browned. (If there is not sufficient fat to achieve this, add 1 tablespoon ghee or oil to help them fry.) Pour the gravy back into the pan and cook, uncovered, until the gravy is thick and a film of oil covers the surface. Serve hot with plain steamed rice and vegetable dishes.

Use 4 tablespoons Charmaine Solomon's Sri Lanka Curry Paste instead of all the Spice ingredients listed above.

Japan, Korea and China

THESE COUNTRIES OF THE Far East offer cuisines that are totally individual. Grouping them in one chapter for geographical convenience will help you discern the differences and enjoy the popular dishes of each country.

Japanese food is different from most other cuisines because it showcases seasonal ingredients. The artistic presentation of even the simplest dish makes it stand apart. Flavours are delicate, encouraging an appreciation of food in its most natural state. Sashimi (raw fish), which used to cause a shudder among westerners, is now appreciated just with its dipping sauce of shoyu (Japanese soy sauce) and a touch of wasabi (green horseradish), and customers are prepared to pay high prices for it.

Not any soy sauce will do when preparing Japanese food. It must be a Japanese shoyu; a Chinese-style or Indonesian-style soy sauce does not

work well. Korea has its own style of soy sauce too, but Japanese soy sauce may be used in Korean food.

The food of Korea is more robustly flavoured, particularly with garlic. It also uses a fair amount of chilli paste and dried chilli, though not in every dish. Beef is the favourite meat, and the popular bulgogi (marinated tender beef strips cooked over charcoal) is what most Korean restaurants specialise in. The basic flavours of Korean food are garlic, ginger, black pepper, spring onions, soy sauce, sesame oil and toasted sesame seeds.

A country as vast as China has thousands of favourite dishes and it is essentially the flavours and textures that distinguish them. The amazing variety of ingredients were probably first used out of sheer necessity and not because of gourmets seeking out unusual foods. Only a small proportion of land is arable, so people have learned to make use of everything edible. Some highly regarded foods are totally devoid of flavour but are prized for their texture. Skilful cooking imbues them with flavour from the seasonings they are combined with. Only the recipes one associates with meals enjoyed in Chinese restaurants or good home cooking are included here for your enjoyment.

Chinese meals do not feature one main dish, but a number of dishes of equal importance. Balance a rich dish with a light one and give vegetables importance, serving them on their own if they are not featured with meat or seafood. Steamed rice is important, the cornerstone of every meal.

Fresh ingredients essential in each of these cuisines include ginger, garlic, coriander and spring onions.

RECOMMENDED PANTRY

Bamboo shoots (preferably winter bamboo shoots), canned
Barbecue sauce
Black beans, canned
Chilli oil
Dashi stock (instant)
Dried shiitake mushrooms
Dried wood fungus
Five-spice powder
Ground bean sauce (*mor sze jeung*)
Hoisin sauce
Korean bean paste (*dhwen jang*)
Korean chilli paste (*gochu jang*)
Mirin (or dry sherry)
Noodles: Japanese buckwheat noodles (*soba*), Japanese wheat noodles (*udon*), potato starch noodles, Chinese egg noodles (*dahn min*), Chinese bean starch noodles (*fun see*), Chinese rice vermicelli (*mi fun*)
Nori (seaweed) sheets

Oyster sauce
Peanut oil
Pickled ginger (*beni shoga*)
Plum sauce
Rice vinegar
Sesame oil (Oriental variety, made from toasted sesame seeds and golden brown in colour)
Sesame seeds (black and white)
Short or medium-grain rice
Shoyu (Japanese soy sauce)
Soy sauce, dark and light (Chinese)
Sichuan peppercorns (ensure they do not contain the shiny black seeds which are gritty when crushed. The reddish brown husks are the fragrant part)
Spring roll wrappers (frozen); if planning a yum cha feast, wonton pastry (available in the refrigerator section of any Asian store)
Star anise
Wasabi (powder or paste)

Chirashi Sushi

For those who like the flavours of sushi but don't have the time to shape and roll it, here's a solution. Chirashi sushi is similar to a rice salad, with as much leeway for adding favourite ingredients.

Serves 6

½ cup cooked crabmeat or prawns
125 g (4 oz) raw fish fillet
1 firm, ripe avocado
6 dried shiitake mushrooms, soaked and cooked as for
      Rice with Chicken and Mushrooms (see page 120)
2 eggs, beaten
salt
1 tablespoon pickled kombu (kelp) in fine strips
1 tablespoon pickled ginger shreds
1 quantity Sushi Rice (see page 116), cooked and cooled

Pick the crabmeat into shreds or thinly slice the prawns.

  With a sharp knife thinly slice the fish.

  Halve the avocado, remove the seed, then slice thickly and peel off the skin. Dice the flesh.

  When the mushrooms have been cooked and cooled, slice very finely.

  Season the eggs with salt and cook into two thin flat omelettes without browning either side. Lay the omelettes on a board and shred them into very fine strips.

  Prepare the Sushi Rice according to the instructions on page 116 and cool. Add all of the ingredients, toss lightly and serve cold.

Sushi Rice

Sushi is rice flavoured with mild vinegar and sugar, formed into small pillow shapes and topped with raw or cooked seafood. Or it may be rolled in a tissue-thin sheet of nori (laver seaweed) or wrapped in a strip of omelette or fried bean curd.

In many of the shops at Sydney's marvellous fish market and increasingly in suburban shopping centres, one finds small take-away sushi places. There are also restaurants devoted entirely to sushi, which seem to have become flavour of the month in many Australian cities. Sushi is not difficult to make at home. While some of the rolled sushi requires a certain amount of care and patience and a flexible bamboo mat to help with the rolling, cone-shaped sushi is easier to form.

Serves 6

500 g (1 lb) short-grain rice
600 ml (20 fl oz/2½ cups) water
5 cm (2 in) piece dried kelp (*kombu*), optional
4 tablespoons rice vinegar
3 tablespoons sugar
2 tablespoons mirin
2 teaspoons salt

Wash the rice in 3–4 changes of cold water and drain in a colander for 1 hour. In a saucepan put the rice and measured water and the piece of dried kelp. Bring to the boil, turn the heat to very low and place the pan on a heat diffuser. Cover with a well-fitting lid and steam for 15 minutes without lifting the lid. Remove from the heat and leave covered for 10 minutes longer. Discard the kelp and turn the rice onto a large flat dish.

If preferred, combine all the ingredients in an electric rice cooker.

Mix the remaining ingredients together, stirring until the sugar is dissolved. Pour over the rice and mix thoroughly. Cool the rice to bring it quickly to room temperature. The seasoned rice is now ready for making sushi.

Sushi with Raw Fish

Moisten hands with cold water mixed with mild vinegar. Take a rounded tablespoon of rice and form into a neat oval shape. These should be no more than two-bite size.

Cut thin slices of very fresh fish that has not been frozen. Spread a thin smear of wasabi on the fish, then place it, wasabi-side down, on the rice. Serve as soon as possible.

Cooked and shelled prawns may also be used for a topping: first cut them almost through the inside curve and spread them so they cover the rice.

Sushi Wrapped in Nori

Toast several sheets of nori on one side, passing them quickly over a gas flame or under a preheated grill. This takes only a few seconds and intensifies the flavour.

Lay a sheet of nori on a bamboo mat or clean napkin and spread ½ cup rice over two-thirds of the sheet. In a row down the centre place strips of raw fish (smeared lightly with wasabi paste), narrow spears of cucumber, pickled radish or soaked and cooked dried mushrooms (as in Rice with Chicken and Mushrooms, see page 120). Roll up using the bamboo mat, enclosing the rice and filling in the sheet of nori. Squeeze gently to press the rice and filling together. Leave to rest for 10 minutes, then cut into slices about 2 cm (¾ in) thick. Arrange on a tray and serve.

For an easier version, make sushi cones. Cut the nori into 12.5 cm (5 in) squares, curl into cone shapes and fill with sushi rice and one or more of the fillings.

NOTE: Fish which is served raw must be impeccably fresh. It is possible to purchase sashimi-quality fish. Tuna, salmon, bonito, kingfish, bream or dhufish are all suitable.

Raw Fish
Sashimi

To be served raw, fish must be impeccably fresh. It is possible to purchase special sashimi-quality fish, and while it is expensive, there can be no compromise. Tuna, salmon, bonito, kingfish, bream or dhufish are all suitable, provided they have been caught the same day and have not been frozen. The quantities are for one serve.

Serves 1

125 g (4 oz) fish, skin and bones removed
1 tablespoon Japanese soy sauce (*shoyu*)
mirin or dry sherry
½ teaspoon prepared wasabi paste
lime juice
1 teaspoon finely sliced spring onions (optional)
1 tablespoon finely shredded white radish (*daikon*)
a few slices of pickled ginger (*beni shoga*)

A sharp knife is essential for removing skin from fish and for slicing cleanly. Handle the fish as little as possible, but make sure there are no bones in it. Cut the fillet into thin slices and arrange on a serving plate, overlapping the slices or curving them into flower shapes. Soft-fleshed fish such as tuna and bonito may be presented in small cubes. Artistic arrangement is part of the appeal of sashimi.

Place a small dish holding *shoyu* or a mixture of *shoyu* and mirin alongside the fish, and also a small mound of wasabi. To eat, mix the wasabi with the *shoyu* for dipping the fish into. If you like, you can add a little lime juice and spring onions for extra flavour. Garnish the plate with the white radish and pickled ginger.

NOTE: Wasabi is also known as Japanese horseradish. Though it is not of the same family as horseradish it has the same pungency. Wasabi is sold in powdered form in small tins, and has to be mixed with cold water and allowed to stand for 10 minutes for its full flavour to develop. Use very sparingly. Wasabi is also sold ready mixed in tubes.

Buckwheat Noodles
Soba

Usually served cold, these noodles make a tasty and light luncheon dish
or snack.

Serves 4

200 g (7 oz) Japanese buckwheat noodles (*soba*)
2 sheets nori
4 small fish cakes (*chikuwa*)
125 ml (4 fl oz/½ cup) dashi
3 tablespoons Japanese soy sauce (*shoyu*)
3 tablespoons mirin or dry sherry
2 teaspoons finely grated fresh ginger or wasabi paste
3 spring onions, very finely sliced

Bring a large pan of water to the boil and drop in the noodles. When the water
returns to the boil add 250 ml (8 fl oz/1 cup) cold water and bring to the boil
again. Cook until the noodles are tender enough to bite—about 2 minutes.
Run cold water into the pan. Drain in a colander and rinse under cold water
2–3 times until the noodles are completely cold. Drain well.

Toast the nori briefly over a gas flame on one side only. With scissors, cut
nori into fine strips or small squares.

Cut the fish cakes into thick slices.

Arrange the cold noodles on individual plates. Scatter nori over the noodles
and place slices of fish cake on the side of the plate.

Heat dashi, *shoyu* and mirin in a small pan. Cool. Pour into individual
sauce dishes. Put small portions of ginger and spring onions on each plate for
seasoning the sauce. Dip noodles into the sauce before eating.

NOTE: Dashi is a light stock flavoured with dried kelp and flaked bonito.
Instant dashi (powder or liquid) is sold in all Japanese stores.

Rice with Chicken and Mushrooms

Serves 6

500 g (1 lb) short-grain rice
8 dried shiitake mushrooms
4 tablespoons Japanese soy sauce (*shoyu*)
4 tablespoons mirin or dry sherry
2 tablespoons sugar
500 g (1 lb) chicken breast fillets, thinly sliced
2 eggs, beaten
a pinch of salt
1 cup cooked green peas

Wash the rice and allow it to drain in a colander for 30 minutes.

Put the dried mushrooms in a bowl, pour boiling water over and leave to soak for 30 minutes or until soft. Save the soaking water, as it retains a lot of flavour and will be used in cooking. Cut off and discard the mushroom stems. Put the caps in a small pan with 125 ml (4 fl oz/½ cup) of the soaking water, 2 tablespoons each of the *shoyu* and mirin, and 1 tablespoon of the sugar. Bring to the boil, cover and simmer until the liquid is almost completely evaporated. Lift out the mushrooms and allow to cool.

In the same pan combine the remaining *shoyu*, mirin and sugar, and chicken. Bring to the boil, turn the heat to very low, cover the pan and simmer for 3 minutes. Remove the pan from the heat and leave covered.

Cook the rice in a rice cooker with 750 ml (24 fl oz/3 cups) water. Or put the rice into a heavy saucepan with a well-fitting lid, add 750 ml (24 fl oz/ 3 cups) water and bring to the boil. Turn the heat as low as possible, cover the pan and cook for 20 minutes without lifting the lid or stirring.

Beat the eggs with salt and use a lightly greased non-stick frying pan to make 2–3 large, flat omelettes. Take care not to brown. Turn each onto a flat plate as they are done. Cut into narrow strips.

When the rice is cooked, spoon into a large casserole or, if you have it, a Japanese *domburi*—a decorative earthenware bowl with lid. Spread the chicken over the rice, and spoon the cooking liquid over. Slice the mushrooms and place over the chicken, then decorate the dish with egg strips and the cooked peas. Serve hot.

120

Grilled Chicken with Teriyaki Marinade

This must be the most universally popular Japanese food—children take to it with gusto, and adults like the combination of salty and sweet flavours.

Serves 6

6 chicken half-breasts, boned but with the skin on
1 clove garlic
2 tablespoons sugar
125 ml (4 fl oz/½ cup) Japanese soy sauce (*shoyu*)
125 ml (4 fl oz/½ cup) mirin or dry sherry
2 teaspoons finely grated fresh ginger
½ teaspoon sesame oil

If preferred, buy a whole roasting chicken and joint it, then bone the breast, legs and thighs.

Crush the garlic to a smooth paste with 1 teaspoon of the sugar.

Combine the remaining sugar, *shoyu*, mirin, garlic, ginger and sesame oil in a large dish and put the chicken pieces into the marinade, turning so they are coated. Marinate overnight if convenient, otherwise leave them for at least 1 hour, turning them over twice.

Cook the chicken under a preheated grill or over a barbecue, brushing from time to time with the marinade. Or preheat the oven to 200°C (400°F). Oil a baking dish and place the chicken pieces in it in a single layer. Roast for 15 minutes, then turn the chicken pieces over with tongs and roast for 10 minutes longer. Spoon some of the marinade over the chicken. Lower the oven to 180°C (350°F) and roast for a further 20 minutes, brushing with marinade twice during this time. The chicken should be glazed and well browned. Cut into bite-sized pieces and serve with rice, or on its own as an appetiser.

NOTE: Fillet steaks (6 small ones) can be marinated in the same mixture, then cooked on a hot, lightly oiled griddle. Heat the remaining marinade in a small pan with 60 ml (2 fl oz/¼ cup) water or dashi, and thicken with 1 teaspoon cornflour mixed with 1 tablespoon cold water. Use as a glaze on the steaks. For eating with chopsticks, slice the steaks and assemble in their original shape.

Sukiyaki

A great dish for table-top cooking. An electric frypan makes a suitable cooking utensil.

Serves 6

1 kg (2 lb) Scotch fillet or other tender, well-marbled beef
125 g (4 oz) fresh shiitake mushrooms, halved,
     or 12 dried shiitake mushrooms
100 g (3½ oz) bean thread vermicelli
12 spring onions, cut into bite-sized lengths
2 medium-sized white onions, cut into eighths
1 small white Chinese cabbage, sliced
1 small can winter bamboo shoots, drained and thinly sliced
vegetable oil for greasing pan
500 ml (16 fl oz/2 cups) beef stock
Japanese soy sauce (*shoyu*)
sugar
sake

Place the beef in the freezer until semi-frozen so it is easy to slice very thinly.

If using dried shiitake mushrooms, soak for 30 minutes in enough hot water to cover. Drain and add 250 ml (8 fl oz/1 cup) of the soaking liquid to the beef stock. (If using fresh mushrooms, just add water.)

Cook the bean thread vermicelli in boiling water for 10 minutes, drain and cut into short lengths.

Arrange the beef, spring onions, mushrooms, onions, cabbage and bamboo shoots on a serving platter, with the vermicelli in a bowl. Have the oil, stock, *shoyu*, sugar and sake close at hand as they will be needed for cooking the sukiyaki.

Heat the frying pan and lightly oil the cooking surface. Add half of each kind of vegetable and fry, stirring, on high heat for a couple of minutes. Push to one side of the pan and add the beef in one layer. After 1 minute, turn and cook the other side. Sprinkle with *shoyu*, sugar and sake according to taste. Add some stock to moisten all the meat and vegetables. Mix in the noodles and heat through. Serve immediately, with each person helping themselves from the pan. Turn off the heat until this has been eaten. When diners are ready for second helpings, heat the pan again and repeat the procedure. Steamed rice may be offered with sukiyaki.

Beef with Sesame Sauce
Shabu Shabu

The Japanese version of this popular combination is cooked in stock at the table. Each diner swishes thin slices of steak briefly in boiling stock, then dips them in sesame sauce. Four is a manageable number of diners, since everyone has to use the pot.

Serves 4

500 g (1 lb) fillet steak
½ Chinese cabbage, sliced
6 spring onions, cut into bite-sized pieces
250 g (8 oz) button mushrooms, halved or quartered
1.5 litres (3 pints/6 cups) beef or chicken stock

Sesame Sauce
3 tablespoons sesame seeds
1 tablespoon white vinegar
125 ml (4 fl oz/½ cup) Japanese soy sauce (*shoyu*), salt-reduced if preferred
2 tablespoons finely chopped spring onions
1 teaspoon finely grated fresh ginger

Trim any fat from the steak and place in a freezer until half-frozen and just firm. Use a sharp knife to cut the meat into very thin slices.

Arrange the cabbage, spring onions, mushrooms and meat on a platter, cover and refrigerate.

To make the Sesame Sauce, lightly brown the sesame seeds in a dry pan over moderate heat, stirring constantly or shaking the pan for even browning, about 5 minutes. As soon as the sesame seeds are golden brown, turn them onto a plate to cool so they don't continue to cook in the heat of the pan.

Ideal for crushing the sesame seeds is a wooden pestle used with a Japanese bowl called a *suribachi*, which has a ribbed inner surface. A mortar and pestle may be used, or even a blender. Add all the ingredients and blend for a few seconds.

At serving time, place a table-top cooker filled with hot stock in the centre of the table and provide diners with bowls, wooden chopsticks and small sauce bowls. A bowl of steamed rice is also a usual accompaniment.

To eat, slices of beef are picked up and suspended briefly in the hot stock, just until pale pink, then dipped in the sesame sauce and eaten with rice. Vegetables, too, are lightly cooked and should be slightly crisp. When all the meat and vegetables are eaten, the stock is ladeled into bowls and, in Japanese fashion, lifted to the lips using both hands.

123

Japanese Pork Cutlet
Tonkatsu

This is a simple and satisfying dish that does not take a great deal of preparation. Ask your butcher for a cut of pork suitable for quick cooking. Butchers are pretty independent and call cuts of meat by names that are not traditional—for example, slices of pork neck are sometimes labelled 'Scotch fillet', which is normally associated with beef. Pork fillet or bolar blade would do as well, if cut thinly as for schnitzel.

Serves 4

4 slices lean boneless pork
3 tablespoons Japanese soy sauce (*shoyu*)
3 tablespoons mirin or dry sherry
1 clove garlic, crushed
½ teaspoon Japanese pepper (*sansho*), or ground black pepper
1 egg, beaten
2 tablespoons finely chopped spring onions
1 cup soft white breadcrumbs
oil for shallow-frying
shreds of pickled ginger for serving

Beat the pork slices slightly to ensure they are thin.

Mix together the *shoyu*, mirin, garlic and *sansho* and turn each slice of pork in the marinade to coat both sides. Leave to marinate for 30 minutes.

Beat the egg well and mix in the spring onions. Have the beaten egg in one large deep plate and the breadcrumbs in another. Dip each slice of pork first in the beaten egg and then in the breadcrumbs, pressing them firmly on both sides. Cover and chill for at least an hour.

When ready to cook heat a large, heavy frying pan and pour in sufficient oil to cover the base of pan. When the oil is hot add the crumbed pork and cook quickly over medium heat until golden brown on both sides, turning once during cooking. Depending on the size of the pan it may be necessary to cook the pork in two batches. Do not crowd the pan. Lift out with tongs and drain on absorbent paper. Cut each piece into strips and assemble the strips in the original shape.

Serve on steamed rice and garnish with pickled ginger. If liked, serve with a tempura-style dipping sauce, which may be bought in a bottle, or mix together 3 tablespoons each of *shoyu* and mirin and stir in 250 ml (8 fl oz/1 cup) of dashi (instant variety) made following the instructions on the packet.

Nine Varieties
Guchulpan

It is easy to see why the dish is thus named—many different fillings are offered to be rolled in pancakes, dipped in sauce and eaten. The traditional serving dish has nine sections in which the nine varieties are arranged.

Serves 6

Pancakes
1½ cups plain (all-purpose) flour
¼ teaspoon salt
2 eggs, beaten
250 ml (8 fl oz/1 cup) milk
250 ml (8 fl oz/1 cup) water
vegetable oil for greasing pan

Filling
sesame oil or vegetable oil for frying
10 dried shiitake mushrooms
soy sauce
ground black pepper
1 teaspoon sugar
3 eggs, separated
250 g (8 oz) beef fillet, finely shredded
3 young carrots, peeled and shredded
salt
12 spring onions, cut into 2.5 cm (1 in) lengths
1 giant white radish, peeled and shredded
250 g (8 oz) zucchini, shredded

Dipping Sauce
175 ml (6 fl oz/¾ cup) soy sauce
3 tablespoons rice vinegar
3 tablespoons crushed, toasted sesame seeds
2 tablespoons finely chopped spring onions

To make the Pancakes, sift the flour and salt into a bowl. Mix the eggs with the milk and water and add to the flour, beating with a wooden spoon until smooth. Or combine in a food processor or blender, strain into a bowl and leave to stand for 1 hour while you prepare the filling.

To cook the pancakes, heat a large frying pan and grease very lightly with oil. Pour in a ladle of the batter and swirl to cover the base of the pan thinly. Cook on medium to low heat so the pancake does not brown. Turn and cook other side, then turn onto a board. When all the batter has been used, cut the pancakes into small rounds with a pastry cutter. Pile pancakes in the centre of the serving dish.

To make the Filling, soak the dried mushrooms in very hot water for 30 minutes. Squeeze out the water, discard the tough stems and thinly slice the caps. Reserve the soaking liquid.

Heat a little sesame oil and stir-fry the mushrooms, then add soy sauce, pepper, sugar and 125 ml (4 fl oz/½ cup) of the mushroom soaking water. Cover and cook for 20 minutes or until the mushrooms are tender and all the liquid absorbed.

Beat the yolks and whites of the eggs separately and cook separately in a lightly greased frying pan to make thin, flat omelettes. Do not have the pan too hot, as they must not brown. Turn out on a board and allow to cool, then shred into fine strips of white and yellow.

Heat 1 tablespoon oil in a pan and stir-fry the beef, adding soy sauce and ground black pepper to taste. Cook till browned and all the liquid has evaporated.

Cook the vegetables separately. The aim is to keep the natural colour of the vegetables, so do not let them brown. Stir-fry the carrots in very little oil, adding salt to taste. Briefly stir-fry the spring onions. Stir-fry the radish until wilted, then season with salt. Stir-fry the zucchini for a few minutes, and season with salt.

To make the Dipping Sauce, combine the ingredients and divide among individual sauce bowls which are placed in front of each diner.

Arrange all the filling ingredients in separate piles around the edge of a plate, with the pancakes in the middle. Set each place with a flat plate, chopsticks and small bowl of sauce. To eat, fill a pancake with one or more of the fillings, roll it up and dip it in the sauce.

Stir-fried Mixture
Chap Chye

For this dish, use Korean potato starch noodles which are springy in texture and need about 8 minutes cooking. Bean thread vermicelli, which are more easily obtainable, may be substituted.

Serves 6

250 g (8 oz) fillet or rump steak, thinly sliced
1 tablespoon soy sauce
1 teaspoon sugar
2 finely chopped spring onions
2 teaspoons finely chopped garlic
1 tablespoon toasted and ground sesame seeds
½ teaspoon ground black pepper
1 tablespoon sesame oil
2 tablespoons dried wood fungus
250 g (8 oz) sweet potato starch noodles (*dang myun*)
salt
3 tablespoons peanut oil
1 red capsicum, finely shredded
6 spring onions, diagonally cut into bite-sized lengths
2 teaspoons Korean chilli bean paste (*gochu jang*) (optional)

Marinate the beef in a mixture of the soy sauce, sugar, spring onions, garlic, sesame seeds, pepper and sesame oil. Set aside for 30 minutes.

Soak the wood fungus in warm water for 20 minutes and cut into bite-sized pieces, discarding any tough bits.

In a large pot of lightly salted boiling water cook the noodles until tender. Drain in a colander, run cold water over them and drain once more.

Heat a wok, add half of the peanut oil and stir-fry the vegetables until just tender. Remove from the wok, add remaining peanut oil and on high heat fry the marinated beef for about 3 minutes, until the colour changes. Add the noodles and mix well, then return the vegetables and toss until combined. If liked, add Korean chilli bean paste to the pan and mix through the noodles.

Korean Barbecued Beef
Bulgogi

In Korean homes and restaurants, a dome-shaped grill is placed over a table-top cooker and each diner cooks his or her own. A small hibachi may be used, or place fine-mesh wire over a standard barbecue so the small pieces of meat don't fall through the bars.

Serves 6

1 kg (2 lb) lean fillet or rump steak, thinly sliced

Marinade
60 ml (2 fl oz/¼ cup) soy sauce
60 ml (2 fl oz/¼ cup) water
2 tablespoons finely chopped spring onions
1 teaspoon crushed garlic
1 teaspoon finely grated ginger
2 teaspoons sugar
¼ teaspoon freshly ground black pepper
1 tablespoon toasted, crushed sesame seeds

Sauce
60 ml (2 fl oz/¼ cup) soy sauce
1 tablespoon sesame oil
2 teaspoons Korean chilli bean paste (*gochu jang*) (optional)
2 tablespoons rice wine or dry sherry
1 tablespoon toasted, ground sesame seeds
2 teaspoons finely chopped spring onions
½ teaspoon crushed garlic
2 teaspoons sugar

Beat out the beef slices until very flat. Trim into bite-sized squares.

To make the Marinade, combine ingredients and pour over the beef and marinate for 3 hours. The best way to cook this is to grill briefly over glowing coals.

To make the Sauce, combine all the ingredients and pour into individual sauce dishes.

Serve the beef with plain steamed rice and the sauce.

129

Steamed Rice

Short- or medium-grain rice is most commonly used in China. Long-grain rice such as jasmine is a popular option in western countries, where restaurants cater to a preference for more separate grains, though fluffy rice not as easy to eat with chopsticks. If long-grain rice is stipulated in any recipe, it is best to use Carolina or jasmine rice and not basmati. The way to cook rice Chinese style is by the absorption method, which makes the grains cling together, although each grain is well defined.

Serves 4–6

500 g (1 lb) medium-grain rice
750 ml (24 fl oz/3 cups) water

Wash the rice in 2–3 changes of water and drain well. Put the rice into a saucepan with the measured water (hot or cold, it does not matter). Bring to the boil over high heat and boil rapidly for 1 minute. Reduce the heat to medium and cook uncovered for 2–3 minutes, without stirring, until holes appear in the surface of the rice, giving a dimpled effect. Cover the pan with a well-fitting lid, reduce the heat to as low as possible and cook for a further 10 minutes without lifting the lid. Turn off the heat and leave the pan covered for a further 10 minutes.

An electric rice cooker is a convenient appliance since it cooks rice and keeps it hot for hours. Use the same proportion of rice to water, but it must be cold water.

Rice Congee

A comfort food if ever there was one, this rice porridge is eaten at any time of day or night, for breakfast, lunch or late supper. Late-night revellers or gamblers seeking consolation are known to partake of a bowl of congee. It fills without the richness of many other dishes.

To make congee, 2 cups steamed rice is returned to the heat with 750 ml (24 fl oz/3 cups) hot water or chicken stock. Simmer until the rice has 'blossomed' to form a thin gruel, about 15 minutes.

If starting from scratch, put 4 tablespoons raw rice and 1.25 litres (2 pints/ 5 cups) water into a saucepan and bring to the boil. Reduce the heat to a simmer, partially cover the pan so it does not boil over, and cook for 45 minutes. These quantities are enough for 2 meal-sized portions.

Accompaniments served with congee are many and varied—sliced spring onions, fried shallots, fried garlic and chilli, crispy fried salted fish, fermented black beans, fried peanuts, soy sauce and sesame oil. These tasty items are added in small amounts, as they are intended only to flavour the rice.

Fried Rice

The secret of successful fried rice is to cook the rice as for steamed rice and as soon as it has finished cooking, to spread the hot rice on a lightly oiled baking tray and leave until it is quite cold and firm. Chill overnight if possible.

The additions to fried rice can be as simple as some chopped spring onions and a sprinkling of light soy sauce. Or they can be elaborate, such as pieces of diced cooked pork or Chinese sausage, shredded omelette, diced mushrooms and small cooked prawns. The rice is fried in peanut oil (about 2 tablespoons to 3 cups cold cooked rice) and seasoned with soy sauce and a little sesame oil. Here is a recipe for a vegetarian version.

Serves 4

4 cups cooked rice, cooled (1½ cups raw rice, cooked as per page 130)
2 eggs, lightly beaten
salt and pepper
4 tablespoons peanut oil
3 spring onions, finely chopped
1 teaspoon finely chopped garlic
1 teaspoon finely grated fresh ginger
2 squares firm bean curd, finely diced
2 cups finely diced vegetables (green beans, celery, zucchini, carrots)
1 cup cooked peas
1 tablespoon soy sauce
1 teaspoon sesame oil
4 tablespoons coarsely chopped coriander leaves

Have the rice cooked and thoroughly cooled. Beat the eggs with salt and pepper to taste.

Heat a wok, add 1 tablespoon of peanut oil and swirl to coat the surface. Pour in the beaten eggs and stir until set. Cut into small pieces with the spatula. Remove from wok and set aside.

Heat the remaining oil and when hot throw in the spring onions, garlic and ginger. Stir-fry until they smell fragrant, just a few seconds. Add the bean curd and stir-fry for 1 minute, then add the vegetables and peas and continue to fry, stirring, for a further 2 minutes. The vegetables should be tender but still crisp.

Add the rice, stir and toss until heated through. Sprinkle soy sauce and sesame oil over, add the coriander leaves and egg. Toss to mix well. Serve immediately.

Lettuce Wraps
Sang Choy Bao

The first time I tasted this was in Hong Kong, and the filling was minced pigeon. Luckily, it is not necessary to pursue the elusive bird. Pork and prawns make a delicious substitute, or minced chicken with the addition of one or two chicken livers for richness. All the sauces used for flavouring are readily available at Asian grocery stores, and keep well after opening.

Serves 6

4 dried shiitake mushrooms
2 tablespoons peanut oil
4 tablespoons pine nuts
2 cloves garlic, finely chopped
1 small onion, finely chopped
250 g (8 oz) minced pork
250 g (8 oz) raw prawns, finely chopped
2 teaspoons bean sauce (*mor sze jeung*)
3 teaspoons oyster sauce
1 teaspoon hoisin sauce
2 teaspoons red bean curd
3 teaspoons sugar
5 tablespoons chopped water chestnuts
5 tablespoons chopped bamboo shoots
2 spring onions, chopped
2 teaspoons cornflour (cornstarch)
3 tablespoons cold water
lettuce, washed and dried

Soak the mushrooms in very hot water for 30 minutes. Discard the stems, squeeze out any excess moisture and dice the caps very finely.

Heat the peanut oil in a wok and on low heat fry the pine nuts only until pale golden, about 1 minute. Lift out immediately on a slotted spoon and have absorbent paper ready to drain them on.

In the oil remaining in the wok, fry the garlic and onion, stirring frequently, until soft and golden. Add the minced pork and fry on high heat until no longer pink. Add the mushrooms and prawns and cook for 2 minutes, then add all the sauces, red bean curd and sugar. Stir in the water chestnuts, bamboo shoots, spring onions and the cornflour mixed with cold water until smooth. Stir until the mixture boils and thickens. Remove from the heat and mix in the pine nuts. Place on a serving plate.

Trim the lettuce leaves to form cups and place next to the filling. To eat, spoon the filling into the lettuce cups and wrap up the mixture.

Cloud Swallows
Wonton

There is a distinct resemblance to the beak and tail of a swallow when the pastry squares are correctly folded to enclose the filling. On a more prosaic note, they may be called deep-fried dumplings. One also finds them on restaurant menus under the name of 'fried short soup sweet and sour' when served with the appropriate sauce.

Makes about 40

6 dried shiitake mushrooms
125 g (4 oz) raw prawns
4 spring onions, finely chopped
3 tablespoons finely chopped bamboo shoots
250 g (8 oz) minced pork
1½ teaspoons salt
1 tablespoon light soy sauce
1 teaspoon sesame oil
250 g (8 oz) wonton wrappers
peanut oil for deep-frying

Soak the mushrooms in hot water for 30 minutes. Squeeze out any excess moisture, discard the stems and chop the caps finely.

Shell and devein the prawns and chop till almost a paste, mixing with the spring onions, mushrooms, bamboo shoots, minced pork and seasonings.

Put a half teaspoon of filling in the centre of each wonton wrapper. Moisten the edges of the dough with a finger dipped in water. Fold over to form a triangle, with the points overlapping slightly. Press together to seal. Pull the two bottom corners of the triangle down to meet under the bulge of the filling, and dab with a little of the meat mixture, placing one corner over the other and pressing firmly. Place on a paper-lined baking sheet, leaving a little space between them. If they touch, this pastry is inclined to stick.

Heat the oil in a wok and deep-fry a few at a time over medium heat so the filling has time to cook through, about 2 minutes. When golden, lift out on a slotted spoon and drain on absorbent paper. Serve as an appetiser or as part of a meal, with sweet and sour sauce poured over just before serving.

NOTE: Wonton wrappers may be purchased from the refrigerator section of any Asian store. They are squares of egg and wheat flour pastry, rolled very thinly and cut into precise 8 cm (3 in) squares. They are also used for steamed dumplings. To make, gather the edges of the pastry around 2 teaspoons of filling in a money bag shape. Steam over boiling water for 10 minutes in an oiled steamer.

Noodles

Wheat and Egg Noodles

Noodles made from wheat flour are the most popular in Chinese cooking. Usually sold in 500 g (1 lb) packets, with each packet consisting of 7–8 small bundles. Allow one bundle per person. They may be served boiled or shallow-fried. Unlike rice or bean thread vermicelli, which are sometimes fried straight from the packet, wheat noodles must be boiled before frying.

The packet instructions invariably tell you to drop the noodles into fast-boiling water. Don't! They must be soaked in warm water first to loosen the strands, otherwise the outside of each bundle will cook but the inner strands will stick together and not cook evenly. This can be done while the pan of water is coming to the boil. If the noodles are loose packed, soaking is not necessary. Neither is it necessary for instant noodles.

Drain the noodles, then drop into lightly salted boiling water with a tablespoon of peanut oil added to prevent boiling over. Depending on the width of the noodles, cook for 2–5 minutes. Test frequently. They should be *al dente*.

As soon as they are done, run cold water into the pan to stop the cooking. Drain in a colander and run cold water through to rinse away excess starch. Drain thoroughly.

Soft-fried Noodles

Sprinkle the well-drained wheat or egg noodles with 1 tablespoon peanut oil and 2 teaspoons sesame oil. Toss to distribute the oil, spread the noodles on a large baking tray and leave to dry for about 1 hour.

Heat a wok or large frying pan and when very hot add 3 tablespoons peanut oil. When the oil is very hot, coil the noodles into the pan, making a round or oval cake. Reduce the heat to medium and fry, shaking the pan but not stirring, until the base is golden. Turn the noodles over and add a little more oil, drizzling it down the side of the wok so it gets hot before it reaches the noodles. Cook for a further 5 minutes or until golden, then transfer to a serving dish. Serve as a base for any stir-fried or braised dish.

Fresh Wheat Noodles

These soft, fresh noodles need only the briefest dip into boiling water before draining and using in soups or stir-fries. Or they may be steamed over boiling water for 10 minutes.

Some varieties of wheat noodles, like thick yellow Hokkien noodles, need only to have boiling water poured over them in a bowl and be left for 1 minute before draining in a colander. They may then be stir-fried with other ingredients.

Spring Rain Noodles with Pork

Romantically called 'spring rain noodles', these are also known as cellophane noodles. They are, in fact, bean starch vermicelli, which turn transparent when cooked. The noodles are sold in a net bag containing a number of 50 g (1½ oz) bundles, which is a great idea because you can then use as many or as few as you like. If you buy a 500 g (1 lb) bundle, it is quite a task separating a small amount from the mass.

Serves 4

3 × 50 g (1½ oz) packets bean thread vermicelli
6 dried shiitake mushrooms
1 tablespoon Chinese rice wine or dry sherry
1 tablespoon light soy sauce
125 ml (4 fl oz/½ cup) chicken stock
2 teaspoons cornflour (cornstarch)
2 tablespoons peanut oil
125 g (4 oz) pork, finely diced
4 spring onions, finely chopped
1 teaspoon finely grated ginger
1 red capsicum or 1 large chilli, finely chopped
1 tablespoon chilli bean sauce
fresh coriander sprigs

Snip the threads holding the bundles of bean thread vermicelli and put the vermicelli in a large bowl. Pour boiling water over to cover.

In another bowl soak the mushrooms in hot water. Leave both for 30 minutes. When the noodles are soft and transparent, drain and cut into short lengths with a sharp knife. Squeeze excess moisture from the mushrooms, discard the stems and dice the caps finely.

Combine the rice wine, soy sauce, chicken stock and cornflour in a bowl.

Heat a wok over high heat, add peanut oil and when the oil is hot add the pork and mushrooms, stir-frying until the pork is browned. Add the spring onions and ginger, stir for a few seconds, then add the chopped capsicum or chilli and chilli bean sauce. Cook over medium heat until the mixture is aromatic, about 1 minute. Stir in the cornflour mixture until it boils. Add the vermicelli and simmer, stirring, until the liquid has reduced. Serve at once, garnished with coriander sprigs.

Pot Stickers

Gow jee pastry or *shiao mai* pastry is sold in the refrigerator section of most Asian stores. If you cannot buy the pastry, make it with the following recipe—it is easy to handle.

Makes about 30

Pastry
250 ml (8 fl oz/1 cup) boiling water
2 cups plain wheat flour

Filling
6 dried shiitake mushrooms
4 spring onions, finely chopped
3 tablespoons finely chopped bamboo shoots
375 g (12 oz) minced pork
1½ teaspoons salt
1 tablespoon light soy sauce
1 teaspoon sesame oil

4 tablespoons peanut oil for cooking

To make the Pastry, pour boiling water over the flour in a large bowl. Stir with handle of a wooden spoon. When cool enough to handle, knead the dough well until smooth. If the dough seems sticky, dust your hands with flour. Shape the dough into a 2.5 cm (1 in) cylinder and slice into 30 pieces of equal size. Cover with plastic or a slightly damp cloth to prevent the surface becoming dry.

To make the Filling, combine all ingredients except the peanut oil. Have filling ready before starting to shape the pot stickers.

Roll out each piece of dough to a circle 10 cm (4 in) in diameter. Pleat the edge of half the circle, which will result in a cup shape. Place a teaspoonful of filling in the centre. Press the pleated edge to a straight edge to seal. (If necessary, brush the edges with a little cold water.) Place the dumplings on a tray, leaving space between each so they do not touch. Cover with a damp cloth.

Heat a large, heavy frying pan over a medium heat. Add 2 tablespoons peanut oil and tilt the pan to coat the base and halfway up the side of the pan. This is important. If the pastry touches a part of the pan that is not oiled, it will stick and tear. When the oil is very hot add half the dumplings or as many as will fit in the pan, placing them flat side down and pleated surface up. Fry until golden underneath.

Now for the exciting part. Add about 125 ml (4 fl oz/½ cup) boiling water to the pan, standing well back and using a long-handled ladle because it will spatter and release much steam. Cover the pan immediately and cook on low heat for 5 minutes. Uncover and cook until the liquid evaporates and the pot stickers become crisp and golden brown on the base. Lift them occasionally with a spatula to prevent them sticking too much.

Remove the pot stickers to a plate, clean the pan and cook the remaining pot stickers in the same way. Serve hot, with a dipping sauce. Chinese red vinegar is traditional, but there are those who prefer chilli sauce or soy sauce.

Steamed Scallops

This is one of my favourite dishes. Scallops are delicate and shouldn't be subjected to heat for too long. I buy white scallops on the half shell, preferably without roe.

Serves 4 as an appetiser

½ teaspoon finely grated ginger
1 teaspoon oyster sauce
1 tablespoon Chinese rice wine or dry sherry
½ teaspoon sugar
16 scallops on the half shell
1 spring onion, cut into fine shreds

Combine ginger, oyster sauce, wine and sugar, stirring until the sugar dissolves.

If the scallops have a dark vein around the side, remove this carefully. Marinate the scallops in the marinade for 15 minutes. With a damp cloth, wipe around the shells in case there are bits of grit or shell. Return each scallop to a half shell and drizzle any remaining marinade over them. Scatter shreds of spring onion over the top.

Place 8 scallops in each of two bamboo steaming baskets and place the baskets over a wok of boiling water. Cover with a bamboo lid and steam over boiling water for 5 minutes. Serve at once.

Prawn Toast

These are popular and so easy to make that even a novice can manage to impress.

Makes 24 savouries

6 square slices white bread
300 g (10 oz) raw prawns
½ teaspoon finely grated fresh ginger
½ teaspoon salt
2 teaspoons oyster sauce
2 teaspoons cornflour (cornstarch)
1 small egg, beaten
oil for deep-frying

Leave the bread slices on a wire rack for an hour or more to dry off slightly. Trim off the crusts and cut each slice into quarters diagonally.

Shell and devein the prawns. If using prawns that have been frozen, dry them very well on absorbent paper. Chop them finely. Put the prawns in a bowl and combine with ginger, salt, oyster sauce, cornflour and beaten egg. Add the egg gradually, stopping when the mixture is of a thick spreading consistency.

Spread the bread with prawn mixture.

Heat oil for deep-frying and when hot, put in a few triangles of bread at a time, prawn side downwards. Fry until the bread is golden. Lift out on a slotted spoon and drain well on paper towels. Serve warm.

Braised Ginger Crab

Live crabs are best for any dish, but I know many cooks who would prefer not to kill them. Wrap the crabs in newspaper and place in the freezer for an hour or two, to put them into a cold-induced sleep. They are then quite easy to handle.

Serves 2

1 mud crab or 2 blue swimmer crabs
6 tablespoons peanut oil
1 clove garlic, finely chopped
1 tablespoon finely shredded fresh ginger
2 tablespoons light soy sauce
2 tablespoons Chinese rice wine or dry sherry
3 tablespoons water
4 spring onions, finely sliced

Wash the crabs well. Remove and discard the carapace, gills and stomach bag. Separate the large claws and crack them with a hammer to allow flavours to penetrate. Divide each crab in half or quarters, according to size. Fry them in 4 tablespoons of the peanut oil on high heat until they change colour.

Heat a wok, add remaining 2 tablespoons peanut oil and swirl. On a medium heat fry the garlic and ginger until soft and starting to colour. Add the soy sauce, wine, water and crabs. Cover and simmer for 8 minutes. Sprinkle in the spring onions, cover and cook for 1 minute longer. Serve hot.

Chilli-fried Squid

For this dish I like to purchase large squid tubes. They are already cleaned and their thickness makes it easy to achieve a decorative effect by scoring them. Smaller squid don't provide quite the same effect, and often the inside of the sac needs cleaning out, which I'd rather not bother with. However, in case you have to use whole squid, there are instructions on how to prepare them. Squid taste good if they are not overcooked, since that makes them tough.

Serves 4

500 g (1 lb) large squid tubes or 750 g (1½ lb) whole medium-sized squid
3 tablespoons peanut oil
2 teaspoons finely chopped garlic
2 teaspoons finely grated ginger
6 spring onions, cut into long diagonal pieces
100 g (3½ oz) snow peas or sugar snap peas (optional)
1 tablespoon sweet–hot chilli sauce or 1 teaspoon hot chilli sauce
2 tablespoons light soy sauce
1 teaspoon sugar
2 teaspoons cornflour (cornstarch)
3 tablespoons water

If using whole squid, hold down the head of the squid with the blunt edge of a knife and pull on the body sac. The head and contents of the sac will come away. Cut off the tentacles and reserve, discarding everything else. Cut away the small sharp 'beak' in the centre of the ring of tentacles. Slit the body of the squid lengthways and rinse well. With a paper towel scrub away the filmy membrane inside the sac and the speckled skin on the outside.

If using large squid tubes slit them lengthways to open them flat, and cut each into 2 pieces. Lay on cutting board with the inner surface uppermost. With a sharp knife held at a 45-degree angle, make a series of parallel cuts about 6 mm (¼ in) apart. Make more cuts in the opposite direction so there is a criss-cross pattern which will blossom into a very pretty effect when the squid is cooked. Cut squid into 5 cm (2 in) squares.

Heat the oil in a wok and stir-fry the squid over high heat just until it curls, no more than 1–2 minutes. Remove the squid pieces from the wok on a slotted spoon. Stir-fry the garlic, ginger, spring onions and snow peas if using for 1 minute. Add the chilli sauce, soy sauce, sugar and the cornflour mixed smoothly with water. Stir until the sauce thickens, then return the squid and toss to coat with the sauce. Serve immediately with steamed white rice.

Fried Fish with Hot Seasonings

Serves 4

1 whole snapper or bream, about 750 g (1½ lb)
coarse salt
2 tablespoons Chinese rice wine or dry sherry
2 tablespoons light soy sauce
2 teaspoons cornflour (cornstarch)
1 tablespoon water
1 tablespoon dark soy sauce
1 teaspoon sugar
125 ml (4 fl oz/½ cup) peanut oil
1 tablespoon finely grated ginger
1 tablespoon finely chopped garlic
1–2 tablespoons chilli bean sauce
250 ml (8 fl oz/1 cup) water
4 spring onions, finely chopped

Buy the fish cleaned and scaled, with its head and tail on. Trim the fins with kitchen scissors. Scrub out the cavity with kitchen paper dipped in coarse salt, rinse in cold water and blot with paper towels. With a sharp knife score the flesh lengthways, making parallel cuts about a finger's width apart and almost to the bone to allow seasonings to penetrate.

Combine the rice wine and light soy sauce and pour over the fish to marinate.

Mix the cornflour with water, then stir in the dark soy sauce and sugar. Set aside.

Heat the oil in a wok and when very hot lift the fish from the marinade and fry for about 4 minutes on each side until golden brown. Turn the fish only once when frying. When ready, lift out the fish with a slotted spoon and put on a serving dish.

Pour off the oil in the wok, leaving 2–3 tablespoons. On a gentle heat fry the ginger and garlic, stirring constantly, until the garlic is golden. Add the chilli bean sauce and water. Stir in the cornflour mixture, then add the spring onions. Stir constantly until the mixture comes to the boil and thickens slightly. Pour the sauce over the fish and serve at once with rice.

Hainan Chicken Rice

A meal in a dish, this homely combination of chicken, rice cooked in chicken stock and a couple of sprightly dipping sauces has become a top favourite in many Asian countries. It is particularly popular with travellers seeking sustenance that will not tax their digestive systems. Chicken rice makes the perfect family meal, offering rice, chicken and a soup based on the chicken stock. The recipe looks long and involved, but the preparation is truly simple.

Serves 5–6

1 × 1.5 kg (3 lb) roasting chicken
salt
3 spring onions, chopped
3 sprigs celery leaves
20 whole black peppercorns
3 sprigs coriander
2 teaspoons sesame oil
¼ small Chinese cabbage, finely shredded
light soy sauce
chopped fresh coriander or spring onions (extra)

Rice
500 g (1 lb) long-grain rice
2 tablespoons sesame oil
2 tablespoons peanut oil
1 tablespoon sliced garlic
1 tablespoon chopped ginger
1 onion, finely sliced
2 teaspoons salt

Dipping Sauces
1 tablespoon sliced red chilli
4 tablespoons dark soy sauce
1 tablespoon ground fresh chilli
1 tablespoon finely grated ginger

Cut off and discard the tail of the chicken with the two fat glands on either side. Also discard any obvious fat near the cavity. Rinse the bird well and dry with paper towels, then rub well with salt inside and out.

In a pan just large enough to hold the chicken, bring 2 litres (4 pints/ 8 cups) water to the boil with the spring onions, celery leaves, peppercorns, coriander and 2 teaspoons salt. When the water boils, lower the chicken gently into the pan, breast downwards. Let the water return to the boil and reduce the heat so it just simmers. Cover the pan tightly and simmer for 25 minutes. Remove the pan from the heat and leave for 45 minutes, still tightly covered, for the chicken to finish cooking in the stored heat.

While the chicken is cooking, wash the rice and leave it to drain in a colander. Heat the sesame and peanut oils in a heavy saucepan and on medium heat fry the garlic, ginger and onion, stirring until they are golden. Remove 1 tablespoon of this cooked oil and reserve for one of the dipping sauces. Add the rice to the pan and fry, stirring, until the grains are coated with oil.

Lift out and drain the chicken. Strain and reserve the stock for cooking the rice and for the soup. Rub the chicken all over with sesame oil. Cover with foil and keep warm.

Add 1 litre (2 pints/4 cups) strained chicken stock to the rice and bring to the boil. Stir in the salt, turn the heat to very low, cover the pan tightly and cook for 15 minutes without lifting the lid. Remove from the heat and leave, covered, for a further 10 minutes.

For one dipping sauce combine the sliced chilli and dark soy sauce. For the second dipping sauce, stir together the crushed chilli, ginger and reserved tablespoon of cooked oil.

To make the soup, bring the remaining strained stock to the boil. Add the Chinese cabbage and light soy sauce to taste. Sprinkle chopped fresh coriander or spring onions over.

To serve, carve the chicken into joints or cut in half lengthways and chop across each half into bite-sized pieces. Serve the soup for ladling over the rice if desired, or sipping between mouthfuls. Serve the sauces in individual dishes.

Honey-glazed Chicken

A jointed roasting chicken may be used in this recipe, but if you do this, add the breast (cut in half) halfway through roasting as the white meat needs less cooking time. Using the same joints, for example, wings, drumsticks or thighs, ensures they all cook at the same time. Wings and drumsticks are ideal for picnics or other informal occasions, as they invite being picked up and eaten.

Serves 6

1.5 kg (3 lb) chicken wings or drumsticks
5 tablespoons dark soy sauce
2 tablespoons peanut oil
2 tablespoons honey
1 tablespoon Chinese rice wine or dry sherry (optional)
2 teaspoons finely grated ginger
2 cloves garlic, crushed
2 teaspoons Chinese sesame oil
½ teaspoon salt
½ teaspoon five-spice powder

If using wings, cut off and discard the wing tips. Put the chicken pieces in a saucepan with just enough water to cover and bring to the boil. Drain immediately.

Combine the rest of the ingredients in a bowl, turn the chicken to coat all over and marinate for an hour or cover and refrigerate for longer, turning the pieces over once or twice.

Put the chicken pieces in a large roasting dish and roast in a preheated moderate oven (180°C/350°F) for 45 minutes. Check them after 30 minutes and if the tops are well browned, turn them over with tongs and brush with the marinade. Cool to room temperature.

NOTE: If wings are cut at the mid-joint, these make ideal finger-food appetisers.

White-cut Chicken

A superbly simple recipe, worthy of a free-range or organically raised chicken.

Serves 6

1 x 1.5 kg (3 lb) roasting chicken
4 spring onions, left whole
1 knob fresh ginger
1 teaspoon whole black peppercorns
4 sprigs celery leaves
2 teaspoons salt
3 tablespoons light soy sauce
1 tablespoon sesame oil

Remove any obvious fat from the cavity of the chicken and rinse the bird well. With a sharp knife cut off the tail including the two fat glands just above it, which the Chinese say give an undesirable odour to the meat. Put the chicken in a pot just large enough to hold it. Add cold water to cover the chicken, then remove the chicken and bring the water to a boil with the spring onions, ginger, peppercorns, celery leaves and salt.

Put a stainless-steel spoon into the cavity of the chicken to conduct heat. Gently lower the chicken into the pot, breast down, and let the water return to a simmer. Cover the pot with a well-fitting lid and simmer for 20 minutes, then turn off the heat and leave for 40 minutes without lifting the lid so that it continues to cook in the stored heat.

Have ready a large pan or bowl with cold water and at least 3 trays of ice cubes in it. Remove the chicken from the hot liquid, drain liquid from the cavity and remove the spoon. (Be careful when draining liquid from cavity that it goes back into the pan and not over your hand.) Try to accomplish this without damaging the skin of the bird. Ensure that the chicken is completely immersed in the water and ice, and chill for 15 minutes. Drain the chicken, place in a large bowl and refrigerate, covered, for at least 3 hours. The chilling results in a layer of jellied stock under the skin of the chicken, so when serving remove meat from bones carefully, keeping the skin intact. Or chop the chicken through the bones into bite-sized pieces and arrange on a platter. To keep the jellied stock intact, cover and chill until serving time.

Make a dipping sauce with the soy sauce and sesame oil, and serve with the chicken.

Red-cooked Chicken

Simmering food in liquid that includes a large proportion of dark soy sauce is known as 'red cooking' because of the rich colour the food acquires. A bonus is the resulting sauce, known as a 'master sauce', that may be used over and over again. Refrigerate or freeze the sauce between times in small amounts, ready to add whenever a dish needs a lift.

Serves 6

1 × 1.5 kg (3 lb) roasting chicken
375 ml (12 fl oz/1½ cups) dark soy sauce
375 ml (12 fl oz/1½ cups) water
125 ml (4 fl oz/½ cup) Chinese rice wine or dry sherry
1 knob ginger, sliced
2 star anise
2 cloves garlic
2 tablespoons rock sugar
2 teaspoons sesame oil

Rinse the chicken in cold water. Cut off the tail and the two glands either side of it. Remove and discard the fat from the cavity. Choose a saucepan just large enough to hold the chicken so it will be almost covered with the cooking liquid. Place the chicken in the pan, breast down, and add all the ingredients except the sesame oil. On gentle heat, bring the liquid to a simmer. Cover and simmer on low heat for 15 minutes, then use tongs to turn the chicken over without piercing the skin. Replace the lid and simmer for a further 15 minutes, basting with liquid every 5 minutes.

Remove the saucepan from the heat and leave the chicken in the covered pan for 40 minutes to finish cooking. Lift the chicken onto a chopping board, letting the liquid in the cavity drain back into the pan. Brush the chicken with sesame oil and either carve into joints or cut in half lengthways and chop into pieces through the bone. Assemble the chicken on a serving plate. Serve with some of the cooking liquid as a dipping sauce.

Refrigerate or freeze the remaining liquid. Use for red-cooking other foods and notice how the flavour intensifies each time it is used. Serve with plain steamed rice.

Roast Duck with Chinese Flavours

We're going to cheat a bit by making use of an oven bag to speed up the cooking. The bag also keeps the duck very moist.

Serves 4–5

1 roasting duck, about 1.8 kg (3½ lb)
2 tablespoons light soy sauce
2 tablespoons hoisin sauce
2 cloves garlic, crushed
2 teaspoons finely grated ginger
1 tablespoon honey
1 tablespoon smooth peanut butter
1 teaspoon sesame oil

Wash the duck and dry on paper towels. Cut off the tail and the oil glands on either side of it. Combine the remaining ingredients and rub some of the mixture both inside and outside the duck, reserving the rest for serving as a sauce.

Put the duck into an oven bag, following the manufacturer's directions about making a few holes in the bag. Leave the duck to marinate for 1 hour.

Preheat the oven to 190°C (375°F) and place the duck in a roasting pan with the breast down. Roast for 50 minutes, then turn the duck so the breast is upwards. Continue to roast for 1 hour.

Remove the duck from the bag, carve into thin slices and serve hot with the remaining marinade as a sauce. If you serve small pancakes to wrap pieces of duck in with slivers of spring onion, the dish seems almost like Peking Duck, with far less effort.

Stir-fried Beef in Black Bean Sauce

Serves 3–4

375 g (12 oz) lean fillet or rump steak
1 tablespoon canned salted black beans
1 large onion
1 bunch Chinese broccoli (*gai larn*)
2 teaspoons cornflour (cornstarch)
1 tablespoon water
3 tablespoons peanut oil
1 teaspoon crushed garlic
1 teaspoon finely grated ginger

Sauce
1 tablespoon dark soy sauce
4 tablespoons water or stock
1 teaspoon sugar
1 teaspoon sesame oil

Trim any fat from the beef. Freeze until firm enough to cut into paper-thin slices.

Put the black beans into a small strainer and rinse under cold water for a few seconds. Drain and chop on a wooden board or mash with a fork.

Cut the onion in half lengthways, then cut each half into 6 wedges.

Cut the Chinese broccoli into bite-sized pieces and blanch for 1 minute in lightly salted boiling water. Drain immediately.

Mix the cornflour and water until smooth.

In another bowl, combine the sauce ingredients.

Heat a wok until very hot, add 1 tablespoon of peanut oil and swirl to coat the cooking surface. Stir-fry the onion for 1 minute. Remove and set aside with the blanched Chinese broccoli.

Add another tablespoon of peanut oil to the wok and when very hot, stir-fry the beef over high heat, tossing until all surfaces come in contact with the pan and look cooked. Push the meat to one side, heat the remaining tablespoon of oil, add the garlic and ginger and stir for a few seconds until they smell fragrant. Add the black beans and fry, stirring, for a few seconds more. Add the sauce mixture and when it boils add cornflour and stir until sauce thickens. Add the onion and Chinese broccoli, toss together to heat through and coat with the sauce. Serve immediately with steamed rice.

Barbecued Pork Spareribs

Look for spareribs that are nice and lean, sometimes called 'American style'. This is a great dish for barbecues, since picking them up with the fingers is the best way to enjoy them.

Serves 6–8

1.5 kg (3 lb) pork spareribs
2 cloves garlic
1 teaspoon salt
1 teaspoon finely grated ginger
2 tablespoons light soy sauce
1 tablespoon dark soy sauce
1 tablespoon honey
1 tablespoon Chinese rice wine or dry sherry
½ teaspoon five-spice powder

Cut the rack of bones into lengths of 4 bones each or, if you have a friendly butcher, ask him or her to do this for you. With a sharp knife, cut between the bones but do not separate them. This enables the marinade to coat more surfaces than if the bones were joined together.

Crush the garlic with the salt to form a smooth purée. Mix with the ginger and all the other ingredients, and brush over the spareribs and between them. Leave to marinate for at least 30 minutes.

Cook at a moderate distance from the heat source over a gas or coal-fired barbecue, until the ribs are golden brown and touched with dark spots here and there.

Or, preheat the oven to 200°C (400°F). Place a rack in a roasting pan (or across the top of the pan) and pour some hot water into the pan so drips from the pork don't burn. Water should not touch the rack. Place the marinated spareribs on the rack and cook in the hot oven for 20 minutes, then turn ribs over using tongs. Reduce the heat to 180°C (350°F), and cook for a further 25–30 minutes or until the spareribs are browned and glazed. Allow extra cooking time if necessary.

Pork in Chilli Bean Sauce

Pork spareribs with their alternate layers of lean and fat need a hot or piquant sauce to balance their richness. The amount of chilli bean sauce may be adjusted to taste.

Serves 4

500 g (1 lb) meaty pork spareribs
1 tablespoon dark soy sauce
1 tablespoon Chinese rice wine or dry sherry
1 teaspoon cornflour (cornstarch)
1 tablespoon water
3 tablespoons oil
100 g (3½ oz) small snow peas or sugar snap peas
2 spring onions, finely sliced
1 clove garlic, finely chopped
2 teaspoons finely chopped fresh ginger

Sauce
1 tablespoon hoisin sauce
2 tablespoons Chinese rice wine or dry sherry
1 tablespoon smooth bean paste (*mor sze jeung*)
1 tablespoon dark soy sauce
2 teaspoons chilli bean sauce
2 teaspoons sugar
2 teaspoons sesame oil

Remove the skin from the spareribs. Cut the pork into thin slices and pour over the soy sauce and sherry, mixing well.

Combine the Sauce ingredients in a bowl, stirring to dissolve the sugar.

In a small bowl, mix the cornflour and water.

Heat the wok, add 2 tablespoons of oil and swirl to coat. When the oil is hot add the snow peas and spring onions and stir-fry for 1–2 minutes. Lift out with a slotted spoon.

Add the remaining tablespoon of oil and fry the garlic, ginger and marinated pork, pressing the pork against sides of wok and stir-frying until fragrant. Pour in the combined Sauce ingredients, stirring well. Cover and simmer for 15 minutes or until tender. Add the snow peas and spring onions, tossing to mix. Serve at once, with steamed rice.

NOTE: Hoisin sauce, bean paste and chilli bean sauce are sold in all Chinese stores and are useful additions to your pantry.

155

Crisp-fried Pork with Sweet and Sour Sauce

Almost a cliché in the world of Chinese restaurants, but there's no denying that many westerners love this dish. I have tried to reduce its richness by using lean pork and, instead of coating the pork with batter, the marinated pork is dipped in a dry flour mixture. After coating with batter or flour, it is fried twice for optimum crispness.

Serves 4–5

500 g (1 lb) pork fillet or other lean, boneless pork
1 tablespoon light soy sauce
2 teaspoons Chinese rice wine or dry sherry
½ teaspoon salt
½ teaspoon ground black pepper
½ teaspoon five-spice powder
1 egg yolk, beaten
1 teaspoon sesame oil
2 teaspoons cornflour (cornstarch)
peanut oil for deep-frying
3 tablespoons plain flour
3 tablespoons cornflour (cornstarch), extra
1 small white onion
1 clove garlic, crushed
1 teaspoon finely grated ginger
1 small red capsicum, diced
1 cup diced fresh pineapple or canned pineapple pieces
3 tablespoons diced water chestnuts (optional)

Sauce
1 tablespoon light soy sauce
1 tablespoon Chinese rice wine or dry sherry
3 tablespoons tomato ketchup
1 tablespoon white vinegar
2 tablespoons white sugar
200 ml (7 fl oz) water or pineapple juice
1 tablespoon cornflour (cornstarch)
1 tablespoon water
2 teaspoons sesame oil

Trim any fat from the pork. Pound the pork all over with the blunt edge of a chopper to tenderise. Cut into 2 cm (¾ in) slices, and the slices into 2 cm (¾ in) cubes. Put the pork into a bowl with the soy sauce, rice wine, salt, pepper and five-spice powder. Mix well. Combine the beaten egg yolk, sesame oil and 2 teaspoons cornflour, pour over the pork and stir to coat the meat. Cover and set aside for 30 minutes or refrigerate for longer.

Heat a wok, add about 500 ml (16 fl oz/2 cups) oil for deep-frying and heat. Combine the plain flour and cornflour in a bag and shake the pieces of pork until they are coated with the flour mixture. Shake off any excess flour and fry the pork in batches for 2 minutes per batch, stirring constantly to keep the pieces from sticking together. Lift out on a slotted spoon and drain on absorbent paper.

To make the Sauce, stir together in a small non-reactive saucepan the soy sauce, rice wine, tomato ketchup, vinegar, sugar and water or pineapple juice. Bring to the boil, stirring. Mix the cornflour with cold water until smooth, and stir into the sauce mixture with the sesame oil. Let it boil for 1 minute or until the sauce is thick and clear. Do this ahead if it's more convenient.

Peel the onion and cut into quarters, then cut each quarter in half crossways and separate the layers. Heat a wok, add 2 tablespoons peanut oil and stir-fry the onion, garlic, ginger and red capsicum for 2 minutes on high heat. Add to the sauce with the pineapple and water chestnuts and heat through.

Reheat the oil and fry the pork for a second time on high heat, for 1 minute. Transfer the pork to a serving dish. Spoon over the sauce and serve at once, with steamed rice.

NOTE: For those who want a sweet and sour pork as they remember it from their favourite restaurant, coat the pork with batter, made by mixing 1 cup plain flour with 125 ml (4 fl oz/½ cup) lukewarm water and 1 tablespoon peanut oil. Allow batter to stand for 30 minutes. Just before using, fold in the stiffly beaten white of one egg. Dust the pork lightly with cornflour (cornstarch) and shake off any excess. Dip the pork in batter.

Make sure the oil is hot enough before frying the pork in batches, taking care not to crowd the pan. Drain on absorbent paper. Bring the oil to high heat before the second frying, which should only take 1 minute.

Grandmother's Bean Curd
Ma Po Dou Fu

One of the famous dishes using bean curd, which the Chinese call 'the meat without a bone' because it is high in protein.

Serves 4

500 g (1 lb) firm bean curd, cut into 2 cm (¾ in) dice
3 tablespoons peanut oil
1 tablespoon finely chopped garlic
1 tablespoon finely chopped ginger
3 tablespoons chopped spring onions
125 g (4 oz) minced pork
250 ml (8 fl oz/1 cup) pork or chicken stock
1–2 teaspoons chilli bean sauce
1 tablespoon ground bean sauce (*mor sze jeung*)
2 tablespoons sweet chilli sauce
2 level teaspoons cornflour (cornstarch)
1 tablespoon water
2 teaspoons dark sesame oil
1 teaspoon chilli oil (optional)
½ teaspoon Sichuan peppercorns

Drop the bean curd into a pan of boiling water and boil for a few minutes to heat through. Drain in a colander.

Heat a wok, add the peanut oil and fry the garlic, ginger and spring onions over a medium heat until fragrant. Add the pork and stir-fry, pressing it against the side of the wok until it is no longer pink.

Mix the stock and sauces together and pour into the wok. Simmer for 5 minutes. Mix the cornflour with water and stir into the sauce until it boils and thickens.

Drop the bean curd into the simmering sauce and stir gently. Add sesame oil and chilli oil and sprinkle with Sichuan pepper. Serve over steamed rice.

NOTE: Roast Sichuan pepper in a dry pan over low heat for 5 minutes or until it smells fragrant. Crush in a mortar and pestle or with a rolling pin, first separating and discarding any shiny black seeds.

158

Braised Mushrooms

These are most useful to have around, as a few can be sliced or chopped and added to rice or noodles to give magnificent flavour. They are also a vegetable dish on their own or may be served as part of a cold hors d'oeuvres platter.

Serves 4

125 g (4 oz) dried shiitake mushrooms
500 ml (16 fl oz/2 cups) very hot water
2 tablespoons dark soy sauce
2 tablespoons sugar
1 tablespoon sesame oil
3 tablespoons peanut oil

Wash the mushrooms briefly in cold water. Put into a bowl, pour hot water over and soak for 20–30 minutes. The better the quality of mushrooms, that is, the thicker the caps, the longer soaking they will need. Use a sharp knife to cut off and discard the stems. Squeeze as much moisture as possible from the mushrooms, reserving the soaking liquid, for it has a lot of flavour.

Stir soy sauce, sugar and sesame oil into 375 ml (12 fl oz/1½ cups) of the mushroom soaking water, stirring to dissolve the sugar.

Heat the peanut oil in a wok and fry the mushrooms over high heat, stirring and pressing them against the hot wok until the undersides are browned. Add the liquid, lower the heat, cover and simmer for approximately 30 minutes or until all the liquid is absorbed and the mushrooms are glazed with the syrupy reduction. Towards the end of the cooking time, stir occasionally. Serve hot or cold.

Green Vegetables in Oyster Sauce

At lunch, dinner or yum cha one of the popular dishes is simply boiled Chinese broccoli (*gai larn*) or asparagus, served with oyster sauce.

Serves 4

1 bunch Chinese broccoli (*gai larn*) or 2 bundles asparagus
1 tablespoon peanut oil
2 tablespoons oyster sauce
1 teaspoon sugar

Wash the vegetables. Trim off mature stems and leaves, keeping only the tender portions. Tie into a bundle with string. If using asparagus, snap off the tough ends.

Bring plenty of water to a rolling boil in a wok. Add the peanut oil. Drop in the vegetables, return the water to the boil and cook for 2 minutes or until the Chinese broccoli or asparagus are tender but still crisp.

Lift the vegetables out of the water onto a board and cut into bite-sized lengths. Arrange on a serving dish. Discard the cooking water.

Put 3 tablespoons of water in the wok, stir in the oyster sauce and sugar and bring to a boil. Pour over the vegetables and serve right away.

Sichuan Eggplant

This dish is almost like a relish, and may be served hot or cold with steamed rice and other dishes. The eggplant keeps well in a glass jar in the refrigerator.

Serves 6 as a side dish

1 kg (2 lb) eggplant
peanut oil for deep-frying
2 teaspoons finely grated ginger
2 teaspoons finely chopped garlic

Sauce
4 tablespoons dark soy sauce
2 tablespoons Chinese vinegar
1 tablespoon Chinese rice wine or dry sherry
2 tablespoons sugar
1 teaspoon sesame oil
1 teaspoon chilli oil
2 teaspoons chilli sauce

Cut the stems off the eggplant and discard. Wash and dry the eggplant well. Cut in half lengthways, then into thick slices. Divide the slices into 5 cm (2 in) lengths.

Heat some peanut oil in a wok and fry the eggplant in 2 batches on high heat, turning them so they are browned on all sides. Lift out with a slotted spoon and drain on absorbent paper. When all the eggplant pieces have been fried, set them aside to cool. The oil may be strained and used again. Leave about 1 tablespoon of oil in the wok.

Combine all the sauce ingredients, stirring until the sugar dissolves.

Heat oil in wok and fry the ginger and garlic, stirring until they are golden. Add the sauce mixture, bring to a boil, then return the eggplant and cook over a high heat, turning the eggplant until most of the sauce is absorbed. Transfer to a serving dish as soon as cooking is completed. Serve warm or cold.

Almond Bean Curd

This only looks like bean curd, but is a simply made, refreshing dessert to follow a Chinese meal.

Serves 6

1 litre (2 pints/4 cups) water
4 teaspoons powdered agar-agar
1 x 400 ml (13 fl oz) sweetened condensed milk
1–2 teaspoons almond essence

Put the water in a saucepan, sprinkle agar-agar over the surface and bring to the boil. Simmer and stir until the agar-agar is completely dissolved. Remove from the heat, add the condensed milk and almond essence and stir well. Pour into a large, shallow glass dish to cool and set. Agar-agar will set without refrigeration but the dessert benefits from being chilled.

To serve, cut into cubes or diamond shapes and serve either on its own or with fruit such as canned longans or lychees, or small melon balls.

Curry Powders and Pastes

CURRY POWDERS or curry pastes? It depends on you and how much time you have to spend preparing meals.

The advantage of using powders is that they don't have to be refrigerated. Just keep them in airtight glass jars, out of sunlight. The disadvantage of using powders is that when you prepare a meal you still have to chop the onions, garlic and ginger and cook them very slowly and thoroughly before you add the spices.

When you've taken the time to make the pastes, the actual preparation of the meal is much quicker because they already contain the onion, garlic, ginger, lemongrass, galangal and other fresh ingredients.

Unless you're a dab hand with the mortar and pestle (stout and heavy, not one of those dainty little ornamental things), a powerful electric blender is the best way to achieve fresh-tasting curry pastes which offer the rewards of making them yourself. No MSG, no artificial colours, no preservatives. You have total quality control. A food processor does not get quite as fine a result as a blender, but may be used if no blender is available.

Store the paste in an absolutely clean glass jar with a tight-fitting lid in the refrigerator. Once you have tasted the results of these recipes you will probably never be satisfied with commercial products.

A Note about Charmaine Solomon's Spice Blends

Our curry pastes and marinades have that home-made aroma and flavour that comes from a carefully balanced blend of top-quality ingredients.

Aware of how little time people have to spend preparing meals, my husband, Reuben, and I have become enthusiastic makers and users of curry pastes. Why don't we just buy them? The answer is simple—we can't find ones that taste right. The pastes and marinades sold under our names are made to the same recipes I'm offering you in this book. They are bottled at a high temperature, which guarantees shelf life without refrigeration until the jar is opened. This temperature cannot be reached without a commercial steam-jacketed kettle.

Always store your freshly made paste, or an opened jar of our paste, in the refrigerator. Use a clean dry spoon to remove what you need, and the rest of the paste should stay perfectly good for at least three months.

Quick Smart Ideas

Once you've made up a supply of curry pastes, or have purchased our pastes, there are many ways you can use them apart from the recipes in this book or those on the label. Here are some ideas to start you off.

Thai Chicken Cakes
Stir 1 tablespoon Thai Red Curry Paste into 3 tablespoons coconut milk and mix into 500 g minced chicken. Add a tablespoon of chopped basil or a few shreds of kaffir lime leaf. Take teaspoonfuls and roll into balls. Grill under a preheated griller or pan-fry in a heavy pan sprayed with olive oil. Or heat just enough oil to cover the base of the pan. Fry on moderate heat until golden all over. For a low-fat version, drop them into non-stick mini-muffin pans and bake in a moderately hot oven for 10 minutes. Serve warm or at room temperature with a sweet chilli sauce for dipping.

Thai Stir-fried Noodles
Add a generous tablespoon of Thai Red Curry Paste to 2 tablespoons of oil in which sliced vegetables, meat or chicken are to be fried. Add cooked, drained bean starch noodles, toss, and distribute the curry paste evenly through the dish. Scatter chopped spring onions or coriander on top.

Spicy Roast Chicken
Rub a roasting chicken or chicken thigh cutlets with Butter Chicken Marinade or Pepper, Garlic and Coriander Paste. Leave for 30 minutes, or overnight in the refrigerator. Roast in a moderately hot oven until done. Serve with crusty bread and salad, or steamed rice and vegetables.

Stir-fried Vegetables
Slice mushrooms or other vegetables and stir-fry in a tablespoon of oil mixed with a tablespoon of one of the curry pastes. Cover and cook for a few minutes.

Stuffed Calamari Tubes
Mix 2 teaspoons Thai Green Curry Paste into 750 g minced pork. Fill calamari tubes. Fasten opening with wooden toothpicks, cover and cook over gentle heat until tender. Cool to room temperature, slice and serve.

Quick Mulligatawny
Prepared stock in the freezer is an asset to the cook in a hurry. Stir 2 tablespoons Korma Paste or Sri Lanka Curry Paste into 1 litre strong beef or chicken stock and heat through. Add ½–1 cup coconut milk, check seasoning and add salt or lemon juice if necessary.

Galloping Horses
In 2 tablespoons peanut oil, fry 2 tablespoons Pepper, Garlic and Coriander Paste or 2 tablespoons Charmaine Solomon's Thai Barbecue Marinade on low heat until fragrant. Add 500 g minced pork and continue to stir-fry until browned. Add ¼ cup each crushed roasted peanuts and fish sauce, 2 tablespoons palm sugar and 2 chopped red chillies. Cook until no liquid remains. Cool. Put a teaspoon of this mixture on bite-sized pieces of fruit (pineapple, mango or star fruit are suitable). Serve at room temperature. Ideal for parties, as this makes about 50.

Spicy Lamburgers
Add flavour to a burger by mixing 1 tablespoon Korma Paste (see page 98) to every 500 g minced lean lamb. Form into patties and cook over a barbecue, under a grill, or in a lightly oiled frying pan.

Pork Balls with Egg Noodles
Mix 2 tablespoons Thai Red or Green Curry Paste with 750 g minced pork. Form into balls and shallow fry until brown, then add ½ cup water, cover and cook until no longer pink in the centre. Cook egg noodles in boiling salted water, drain well, add to pan with pork balls and mix gently together, stirring in a little extra curry paste or chilli sauce if liked. Serve hot.

Quick Spring Rolls
Mix 1 tablespoon curry paste or Pepper, Coriander and Garlic Paste (or use my Thai Barbecue Marinade) with 250 g pork mince. Shape spoonfuls into cylinders and wrap in small spring roll pastry squares, turning in the sides to enclose. When all are made, deep fry in hot oil until golden. Drain on kitchen paper towels and serve with Nuoc Cham (see page 37).

Ground Spice Mix
Garam Masala

There is more than one version of garam masala, some only using fragrant spices and others including pepper. A freshly made garam masala is so superior to any commercial variety that I strongly urge the keen cook to make some and store it airtight and out of direct sunlight. It will keep its flavour and fragrance for months.

Makes about ½ cup

4 tablespoons coriander seeds
2 tablespoons cumin seeds
2 teaspoons whole black peppercorns
2 teaspoons cardamom seeds
4 small cinnamon quills
1 teaspoon whole cloves
1 whole nutmeg

In a small pan roast *separately* the different seeds until they smell fragrant, shaking the pan or stirring constantly. The larger seeds such as coriander will take longer than the slender seeds of cumin. As soon as each one is done, turn onto a plate to cool.

After roasting, peel the cardamom, discard the pods and use only the seeds. Roasting not only brings out the flavours but also makes the spices easier to grind. Put all the spices except the nutmeg into a blender and grind to a fine powder, or pound in a mortar and pestle. Finely grate the nutmeg and mix in. Store in an airtight container.

NOTE: To peel cardamom pods, first bruise them with the pestle so they split, making it easier to do this chore without ruining your nails.

Sri Lanka Curry Powder

The spices for Sri Lankan curries are dark roasted until about the colour of coffee. Because the spice seeds are of varying sizes they must be roasted separately, otherwise some would burn in the time it takes to cook the others.

Makes about 1 cup

90 g (3 oz) coriander seeds
45 g (1½ oz) cumin seeds
30 g (1 oz) fennel seeds
15 g (½ oz) fenugreek seeds
1 cinnamon quill, about 5 cm (2 in)
1 teaspoon whole cloves
1 teaspoon cardamom seeds
2 tablespoons dried curry leaves
2 teaspoons chilli powder
1 tablespoon ground rice

Roast each of the spice seeds *separately* in a dry pan over low heat, stirring constantly until each one becomes a fairly dark brown. Do not let them burn. Put this mixture into a blender with the cinnamon, broken into pieces, the cloves, cardamom seeds and curry leaves. Blend on high speed to make a fine powder. If your blender is not powerful enough, use a sturdy mortar and pestle to achieve the results. Combine with the chilli powder and ground rice and store in an airtight jar. Use 2 level tablespoons of powder to each 500 g (1 lb) main ingredient.

Whole Seed Mix
Panch Phora

'*Panch*' means five in Hindi and *panch phora* is a combination of five different aromatic seeds. These are used whole, and when fried in oil at the start of a dish, impart an exquisite flavour.

Makes about ¾ cup

2 tablespoons brown mustard seeds
2 tablespoons cumin seeds
2 tablespoons nigella seeds (kalonji)
1 tablespoon fennel seeds
2 teaspoons fenugreek seeds

Put all the seeds into a glass jar with a well-fitting lid. Shake before use to ensure even distribution, as the heavier seeds tend to sink to the bottom.

Pepper, Garlic and Coriander Paste

For anyone who enjoys the flavour of Thai food, this basic flavouring is useful to have in the refrigerator, instead of having to make it each time it is needed.

Makes about 1 cup

about 200 g (7 oz) fresh coriander leaves, stems and roots
1 tablespoon chopped garlic
2 teaspoons salt
1–2 tablespoons whole black peppercorns
2 tablespoons lemon juice

Wash the coriander well, paying particular attention to the roots, which are usually sandy. Chop coarsely and measure about 2 cups, including roots.

Crush the garlic to a smooth paste with the salt.

Roast the peppercorns in a dry pan, stirring constantly, for a minute or until they smell fragrant. Crush coarsely in a mortar and pestle, add the coriander and pound to a paste. Mix in the garlic and lemon juice. Store the paste in a clean, dry screw-top jar in the refrigerator for up to 3 months. Use a clean, dry spoon each time you take some.

Red Curry Paste

See pages 166 and 167 for other ways to use this paste.

Makes about 1 cup

Dried Spices
1 tablespoon coriander seeds
2 teaspoons cumin seeds
1 teaspoon black peppercorns
2 teaspoons paprika
1 teaspoon ground turmeric

Fresh Ingredients
10 fresh or dried red chillies
10 small purple shallots or 2 small brown onions, roughly chopped
5 large cloves garlic
2 stems lemongrass, white portion only, thinly sliced
50 g (1½ oz) galangal, fresh or in brine, roughly chopped
2 tablespoons chopped coriander roots and pale coriander stems
4 fresh kaffir lime leaves
finely grated zest of 1 kaffir lime
2 teaspoons dried shrimp paste
60 ml (2 fl oz/¼ cup) vegetable oil

Lightly toast the spices in a dry pan to bring out the flavours (it also makes grinding them easier). Toast the coriander seeds until fragrant, transfer to a plate. Toast the cumin seeds—they will be done in less time than the coriander as they are much smaller. Add to the coriander. Lightly toast the peppercorns. Grind all three to powder in a mortar and pestle or blender. Combine with the paprika and turmeric.

Seed the chillies if you do not wish the paste to be too hot. If using dried chillies, soak them in about 60 ml (2 fl oz/¼ cup) hot water for 10 minutes. Put into a powerful electric blender with the soaking water and add the shallots, garlic, lemongrass, galangal and coriander roots and stems. Remove and discard the tough mid-rib of the kaffir lime leaves, and put the leaves and zest into the blender.

Wrap the shrimp paste tightly in foil and toast under a hot griller for 2 minutes on each side then unwrap and add to the blender. Add the vegetable oil and ground spices and blend until smooth. The paste may be stored in a bottle in the refrigerator for 3 months, or divided into convenient-sized portions and frozen.

To make meal preparation even easier and quicker, heat an extra 2 tablespoons of oil and gently cook the spice blend, stirring constantly, until it is bubbling and fragrant. This way, it is already cooked and mellowed when you come to use it. Bottle it hot or after it has cooled.

Green Curry Paste

A green curry can be devastatingly hot if prepared the traditional way, using bird's eye chillies. I prefer to use the longer, larger green chillies which deliver less heat, and add just 2–3 of the small bird's eye chillies. When seeding or slicing chillies, use disposable gloves to protect your hands.

Makes about 1 cup

6 large green chillies and 2 bird's eye chillies
1 teaspoon dried shrimp paste
½ cup sliced purple shallots or 1 medium-sized brown onion, chopped
1 tablespoon chopped garlic
1 cup chopped coriander leaves, stems and well-washed roots
¼ cup finely sliced lemongrass, white portion only, or zest of 2 lemons
2 tablespoons chopped galangal, fresh or in brine
2 teaspoons freshly ground coriander seeds
1 teaspoon ground cumin seeds
1 teaspoon ground black peppercorns
1 teaspoon ground turmeric
2 tablespoons vegetable oil

Remove stems and roughly chop the chillies.

Wrap the shrimp paste tightly in foil and toast under a hot griller for 2 minutes on each side and add to the blender.

Put all the ingredients into an electric blender and blend to a purée. Add a little extra oil or water if necessary to make blending easier. Store the paste in a clean, dry screw-top jar in the refrigerator for up to 3 months. Use a clean, dry spoon each time you take some.

Tom Yum Paste

The tom yum of Thailand is based on flavours like those incorporated in this hot and sour soup paste. Use 2 tablespoons paste in 750 ml (24 fl oz/3 cups) of prawn or chicken stock. Shelled and deveined prawns are cooked in the stock until done.

Makes about 375 ml (12 fl oz/1½ cups)

125 ml (4 fl oz/½ cup) vegetable oil
2 teaspoons chilli powder
½ cup small dried shrimp
½ cup finely sliced lemongrass, white portion only, or zest of 1 lemon
1 tablespoon finely chopped garlic
2 tablespoons chopped coriander roots
10 whole peppercorns
1 tablespoon finely chopped galangal, fresh or in brine
4 fresh red chillies, seeded
4 fresh green chillies, seeded
8 fresh kaffir lime leaves, mid-rib removed
4 tablespoons fish sauce
4 tablespoons lime juice
1 teaspoon ground turmeric
1 tablespoon dried shrimp paste
1 tablespoon sugar
1 tablespoon salt
1 tablespoon citric acid
1 teaspoon finely grated lime zest

Heat the oil gently in a wok or frying pan. Mix the chilli powder with 1 tablespoon water and cook until the oil turns red. Turn off the heat while preparing the other ingredients.

Put the dried shrimp into a blender and whiz on high speed until reduced to a fine floss. Transfer to a bowl.

Put the lemongrass, garlic, coriander roots, peppercorns, galangal, chillies and kaffir lime leaves into the blender. Add the fish sauce and lime juice and blend until puréed.

Reheat the chilli oil in the wok and add the puréed mixture. Add the turmeric, shrimp paste and shrimp floss. Cook, stirring, until the oil separates and comes to the surface. Cool the mixture before stirring in the sugar, salt, citric acid and lime zest. Store in a tightly covered glass jar in the refrigerator for up to 3 months, or freeze in 2-tablespoon lots.

Masaman Curry Paste

A paste that shows the influence of Muslim traders, which is why it is named 'Masaman'. It enjoys great popularity in Thailand, and is a true cross-cultural dish, blending two great cuisines. The method and ingredients for this paste are as for Red Curry Paste (see page 173), with the addition of fragrant spices that are typical of the cooking of India.

Makes about 1 cup

Dried Spices
1 tablespoon coriander seeds
2 teaspoons cumin seeds
1 teaspoon black peppercorns
2 teaspoons paprika
1 teaspoon ground turmeric
1 teaspoon fennel seeds or ground fennel
1 teaspoon ground cinnamon
½ teaspoon ground cardamom
½ teaspoon ground nutmeg or mace
¼ teaspoon ground cloves

Fresh Ingredients
10 fresh or dried red chillies
10 small purple shallots or 2 small brown onions, roughly chopped
5 large cloves garlic
2 stems lemongrass, white portion only, thinly sliced
50 g (1½ oz) galangal, fresh or in brine, roughly chopped
2 tablespoons chopped coriander roots and pale coriander stems
4 fresh kaffir lime leaves
finely grated zest of 1 kaffir lime
2 teaspoons dried shrimp paste
60 ml (2 fl oz/¼ cup) vegetable oil

Lightly toast the spices in a dry pan to bring out the flavours (it also makes grinding them easier). Toast the coriander seeds until fragrant, transfer to a plate. Toast the cumin seeds—they will be done in less time than the coriander as they are much smaller. Add to the coriander. Lightly toast the peppercorns. Grind all three to powder in a mortar and pestle or blender. Combine with the paprika, turmeric, ground fennel, cinnamon, cardamom, nutmeg and cloves.

Seed the chillies if you do not wish the paste to be too hot. If using dried chillies, soak them in about 60 ml (2 fl oz/¼ cup) hot water for 10 minutes. Put into a powerful electric blender with the soaking water and add the shallots, garlic, lemongrass, galangal and coriander roots and stems.

Remove and discard the tough mid-rib of the kaffir lime leaves, and put the leaves and zest into the blender.

Wrap the shrimp paste tightly in foil and toast under a hot griller for 2 minutes on each side, take out of foil and add paste to the blender. Add the vegetable oil and ground spices and blend until smooth. The paste may be stored in a bottle in the refrigerator for 3 months, or divided into convenient-sized portions and frozen.

To make meal preparation even easier and quicker, heat an extra 2 tablespoons of oil and gently cook the spice blend, stirring constantly, until it is bubbling and fragrant. This way, it is already cooked and mellowed when you come to use it. Bottle it hot or after it has cooled. Cap tightly and store in the refrigerator.

Stockists

AUSTRALIA

UNITED KINGDOM

UNITED STATES OF AMERICA

CANADA

SWITZERLAND

Index